The Reconciling Parish

A Process for Returning or Alienated Catholics

Patrick J. Brennan

A Resource for Parish Staffs and Leaders

Allen, Texas

Copyright © 1990 by Tabor Publishing, a division of DLM, Inc.

All rights reserved. No part of this book shall be reproduced or transmitted in any form or by any means, electronic or mechanical, including photocopying, recording, or by any information or retrieval system, without written permission of the Publisher.

Send all inquiries to:
Tabor Publishing
One DLM Park
Allen, Texas 75002

Printed in the United States of America

ISBN 0-89505-765-4

1 2 3 4 5   93 92 91 90 89

For my brother,
Bill,
and again in gratitude to
Dawn,
a model of Woman-Church

CONTENTS

Preface	vii
1 Dropout and Alienation Patterns	1
2 A Reconciling Church	11
3 Pastoral Issues	23
4 Principles for a Ministry of Reconciliation	31
5 Ministries of the Reconciling Community	37
6 Synthesis	47
7 Evangelizing Catechesis	67
Study Guide: Remember, Return, and Rebirth	75
Session 1: We believe in the face of mystery.	75
Session 2: We believe in God the Father (Parent), creator of heaven and earth.	78
Session 3: We believe in Jesus, God's Son, our Lord, who was crucified, died, and was buried.	81
Session 4: We believe in the Holy Spirit, the Lord, the giver of life, who proceeds from the Father and the Son.	84
Session 5: We believe in Jesus, born of Mary.	87
Session 6: We believe in one, holy, catholic, and apostolic Church.	90

Session 7: We believe in Baptism
and the other sacraments. 93

Session 8: We believe in the forgiveness of sins. 97

Session 9: We believe in the resurrection of the dead. 100

Session 10: We believe in the life of the world to come. 103

Epilogue: Reflections and Critique from Experience 107

**Appendix: Adapting the RCIA for the
Reconciling Parish Process** 111

Index 117

PREFACE

"Forgetting" and "wandering" are images frequently used in Scripture to describe alienation from God or the community. The Old Testament and the New Testament encourage us to remember God and to return to God. The phenomena of forgetting and wandering are key to understanding the inactive or alienated Catholic in our own day. But it is important to keep in mind that it is not only the inactive member who does the forgetting or wandering. We as a church often forget the inactive and the alienated and wander from them. As briefly referred to in my earlier book, *The Evangelizing Parish,* more and more archdioceses, dioceses, parishes, and clusters of parishes need to engage in a ministry of reconciliation to the inactive and the alienated—not to manipulate them back to church, but rather to communicate care and concern for them.

This book does not repeat material on home visitation contained in *The Evangelizing Parish.* Rather, it begins with the presumption that a group of people have presented themselves as interested in remembering with the parish. Instead of including these people in the Rite of Christian Initiation of Adults, a process for those joining the Church, I am recommending a blending of the RCIA and the Order of Penitents, a process developed from the first to the fourth centuries for the gradual resocialization of interested people and their families into the Body of Christ. The culmination of this process of reconciliation, as for catechumens, takes place during the Easter

Triduum, with a special focus on Holy Thursday. The process follows the patterns of the Order of Penitents. Historically, the Order of Penitents was distinct from the heavily juridical canonical penance, which began in the fourth century.

While several strategies for reconciliation with the alienated or the returning Catholic will be offered, the main one referred to will be the synthesis of the RCIA process and the Order of Penitents, called in this book the reconciling community. The reconciling community is one ministry of reconciliation offered in a faith community that is trying to become a reconciling parish.

It is my firm conviction that greater care and ministry toward reconciliation with hurt or alienated members will result in a genuine rebirth for the Church of Jesus Christ.

1
Dropout and Alienation Patterns

British psychiatrist Jack Dominian summarized the findings of a study of the religious attitudes and practices of European Catholics in the August 3, 1985, issue of the international journal *The London Tablet*. Dominian synthesized the findings of Dr. Michael Hornsby-Smith, a British sociologist. Dominian feels that the European findings are indicative of a movement, or shift, in the entire Church, including the American Church. Dominian spoke of the Catholic Church as now being populated by three distinct churches.

1. First church Catholics. This subpopulation is characterized by traditionalism. First church Catholics are loyal to the pope, the hierarchy, and Catholic tradition. They place few expectations on their parish. They go to church to pray and to worship God. If the celebrant-preacher or the quality of the religious celebration offers them something to think about, that is appreciated. But they can also go to church week after week without the popular expectation that they will "get something out of it." This generation was taught to "bring something" to church, rather than to wait for or to expect the celebrant or someone else to bring something to them. First church Catholics are an aging, dying generation, and are increasingly few in number.

2. Second church Catholics. This subgroup is made up of young-adult, middle-aged, and some older Catholics who are disciples of the Second Vatican Council. The vision, or theology, of Church—and the style of being Catholic advocated by the council—has indeed been embraced by this subgroup. However, this group, spanning at least three generations, is not as large or significant as many Catholics think. Second church Catholics, like first church Catholics, are an aging subcommunity.

3. Third church Catholics. Dominian feels that a new age is dawning in which third church Catholics will predominate the Church. These Catholics—many young adults, some older—are in many ways *culturally* Catholic. The aging first and second churches will continue to be outnumbered by third church Catholics. This subgroup has spiritual hungers and thirsts, but it generally is alienated from the traditional, institutionalized trappings of Catholicism. Also, because of their lack of institutional conditioning, third church Catholics are quite susceptible to the personalist, noninstitutional evangelization strategies of evangelicals and fundamentalists. If the Roman Catholic Church, as well as mainline Protestant churches, is to have any success in reaching out to the third church, it needs to develop a spirit of innovation in evangelizing tactics.

MODERN-DAY TRENDS

In an interesting document entitled *Australia: Facts and Figures,* James M. Fitzpatrick, director of the Catholic Enquiry Center, attempts to give a statistical demographic picture of the Church in Australia. Some of his research reflects similar trends in America. Using statistics, Fitzpatrick articulates the growing need for making evangelization the top priority for the Australian Church. He isolates four major problems that are weakening contemporary believers' sense of the sacred and religious commitment.

1. Growing depersonalization. One of the dangers of rapid growth in business, industry, and technology is depersonalization. This depersonalization in turn is accompanied by feelings of powerlessness, alienation, anxiety, stress, and depression. All of this has created in society a crisis of meaning.

2. Secularization. Materialism and human potential are becoming more and more the foundation for people's lives. Secularization involves not only losing touch with the sacred but also divorcing the sacred from one's day-to-day living. Thus, people may still be churchgoers, but they can leave what they have prayed about or listened to at church and live their lives in ways that are in conflict with the Gospel.

3. Crisis of credibility. Fitzpatrick refers to an "explosion of authorities in contemporary culture," that is, a real plurality of voices and values claiming to be "truth" for life. (On the American scene, we need only look at how posters of pop and rock stars now decorate the rooms of American Catholic youth, rather than some of the symbols of the sacred of bygone years.) The root meaning of the word *authority* is "to give life" or "to author life." Media stars, politicians, and self-help preachers and writers have all found their own pulpits, leading to a crisis of credibility among Catholic people. In short, people are turning to many "authorities" other than the Church or Jesus for guidance and direction.

4. Erosion of traditional values. Change in itself is not evil. In fact, science and technology have contributed much to the advancement of the human family. But the rapid pace of change in the modern world has also weakened some traditionally held values. More and more people are experiencing a devaluing of the family, moral confusion in the areas of sexuality and respect-for-life issues, and a desensitization to the issues of social justice and peace.

While the above material is describing an Australian phenomenon, it is also a summary of trends around the world, and certainly in America.

In the same study, Fitzpatrick attempts to classify types of believers, nonbelievers, and dropouts. Again, his categories are helpful.
- *Non-Christians.* These people have never embraced the person or values of Jesus. Among this group are those who may in fact embrace the values of other faith traditions.
- *Christians.* This group adheres to the traditions and values of Christianity. Within this group are a number of different denominations, as well as a variety of levels of commitment.
- *Post-Christians.* Though baptized, and perhaps culturally Christian, people in this group are little influenced by Christianity. Religion, for them, has become a social convention.

- *Atheists.* People in this group can be described as being antibelief. They look on Christianity as erroneous, an illusion to be refuted.
- *Postatheists.* These people are indifferent to spirituality. They live completely materialistic or humanistic lives. They are functional atheists, without militancy or rancor.

PRACTICES OF AMERICAN CATHOLICS

The significance that the European and Australian analyses have for this study is the degree to which they mirror the practices of American Catholics. In its August 5, 1986, edition, the *Chicago Tribune* carried an article that sums up some of the alienation patterns. In the article, entitled "My Catholicism: Not a Faith, But a Shared History," Donna Quindlen described herself as a "cultural Catholic." Quindlen's self-description is a case study of the third church Catholic: "Catholicism is to us now not so much a system of beliefs or a set of laws but a shared history. It is not so much our faith as our past."

In the typical American parish, the number of "cultural Catholics" is alarming. In the archdiocese of Chicago, for example, two-thirds of the potential congregation in most parishes are not coming to church. Father Thomas Sweetser, S.J., author of *Successful Parishes,* further hypothesizes that around 92 percent of those coming to church can be classified as "active uninvolved"; that is, they basically come to the parish church for sacramental services.

Why People Feel Alienated

In another book, *The Evangelizing Parish,* I documented many reasons that people list for becoming alienated from the parish or from active involvement in the Church. The following summarizes some of that material.
- *Anti-institutionalists.* These people react negatively to the bureaucracy of organized religion.
- *Those who have been hurt by the Church.* Many perceive the Church as having hurt them, either directly, in a personal way, or indirectly, through principles and ideological stands that seem exclusive and judgmental.
- *Those who are in pain.* Dr. John Savage, author of *The Apathetic and Bored Church Member,* has studied these

people extensively. He postulates that they have a cluster of painful situations present in their lives. They leave active membership in parishes that seem unaware of or insensitive to their hurt.

- *Searchers.* These people are still looking for life's meaning and for a community in which to express their faith. Very often, searchers have been culturally reared in a specific faith tradition but have not chosen that tradition as their own.
- *The unconverted.* Similar to searchers, these people have not yet had a significant conversion experience. Unlike searchers, however, they have not yet consciously begun to search for "the more" of an active faith life. The unconverted frequently have been raised in a mainline Protestant church or in the Catholic Church. With such people, parents and ministers alike need to deal honestly with the questions "Have we really lost these people? To what degree did we ever really have them?"
- *The spiritually starving or disappointed.* Some people find their parish or its services unstimulating and transfer their allegiance to another parish, church, or denomination. Others simply drop out and cease looking for spiritual nourishment in the parish or in their church of origin.
- *The secularized.* These people have experienced a shift in their values and attitudes. Their new life-styles often are at odds with Gospel values or regular church membership.
- *The morally searching.* Some people feel that because they engage in a particular type of immorality, they are outside the realm and identity of churchgoer or parishioner. In a sense, they feel they no longer fit.
- *Geographical transplants.* In modern society, many people move from one area to another quite frequently. This nomadic life-style often results in a kind of rootlessness in terms of neighborhood, relationships, and parish commitment.
- *Those reacting to institutionalized sexism and other issues.* There are both men and women who are angry, hurt, and alienated over the apparent secondary role assigned to women by the male-dominated Church. Related to this group are many other people who react negatively to other apparent flaws of the official Church, for example, authoritarianism, doctrinal rigidity, clericalism, hierarchical bureaucracy, and the lack of a positive spirituality of human sexuality.

- *Culture-shock dropouts.* Some people are still angry or hurt about the changes in style of Church that began in the 1960s. This group, especially, has transmitted religious alienation from one generation to another over the last twenty-five years.
- *Marriage-related dropouts.* The marriage of a Catholic to an unchurched person or to an active member of another religion can often influence the religious practice of the Catholic. The Catholic may become lukewarm in his or her own faith practice or gravitate toward the religion of the spouse. Included in this group are the divorced, and possibly the remarried, who may have been made to feel unwelcome at a given parish.

SPECIAL CHALLENGES

There are three rather broad categories of alienated Catholics who need special consideration: the young (children, adolescents, and young adults), the racial or ethnic dropouts, and the uninvolved active members. It will help to describe these groups in a bit more detail.

The Young

Children. Many children have been baptized but never really nurtured in the faith. Some live a kind of "religious schizophrenia"—they are enrolled in CCD or parochial school programs but return to a nonpracticing family context. Others have not had any religious education and are in need of a rite of Christian initiation for children to help them complete their sacramental initiation and growth in faith.

Adolescents. Most teenagers experience a kind of alienation from organized religion. One of the paradoxes of adolescence, however, is that it is a deeply spiritual time in which a young person wrestles with some very heavy issues—identity, sexuality, personal morality, the inevitability of suffering and death, the purpose and meaning of life. Psychologist William James felt that the adolescent upheaval is paradigmatic of what conversion experiences look like and feel like throughout the life cycle, that is, a collapsing of vision, values, hopes, and dreams, followed by struggle and reintegration. Many adolescents find the anonymity, traditionalism, and adult orientation of Sunday worship irrelevant for the struggles that they are experiencing.

Parishes have a responsibility to reach out to as many of their young people as possible. This requires an investment of time, money, and personnel—an investment that is not taking place in many faith communities. Even if a parish is willing to make such a commitment, the influence on young people of other visions, value systems, and spiritualities is often so strong that the parish may not fully succeed in evangelizing its young people. One thing is certain: Without a real commitment to youth ministry, young people are likely to become bored and drop out from parish involvement, or seek other communities to meet their needs.

Young Adults. In *The American Catholic Church*, George Gallup and James Castelli summarize trends and areas of need in the Catholic Church today. According to the authors, one area in which the Church receives "low marks" is ministry to young adults. Many Catholic parishes operate out of a kind of "graduation" mind-set in which the end of CCD or the completion of Confirmation marks the end of a relationship between the faith community and the young person. Some years ago, Michael Warren, in *Youth and the Future of the Church*, described the young adult as spiritual but not necessarily religious. A relationship with organized religion is not one of the needs of the young adult. Rather, young adults are consumed with beginning their adulthood: solidifying identity, finding intimacy, beginning a career, leaving home, finding new roots, and developing support groups and friendships. These are the areas in which young adults need ministry and help from the parish. To welcome back the young adults who have become inactive, the faith community must speak to the needs of young adults. Parish ministry should have as its motif that young adults are a "pilgrim people"—people on the move, people journeying. The faith community must move with them, in their world, in "tent churches" on their own turf.

Racial-Ethnic Dropouts

The July 8, 1985, issue of *Time* magazine spoke of the competition among the various Christian denominations in claiming the spiritual allegiance of Hispanic Americans. In "The Crusade for Hispanic Souls," journalist Richard N. Ostling reports a significant decline in the number of Hispanics actively participating in the Catholic Church. Hispanic immigrants to the United States find the American Church cold, indifferent, and culturally foreign to them. Assembly of God and other proactive evangelizing groups reach out to the Hispanic Catholic, offering friendship, membership in a small faith community, and possibly leadership roles. The typical Catholic reactive stance, as opposed to the proactive evangelizing strategies of other groups, has allowed these groups to "rustle" Hispanic Catholic congregations over to other faith expressions. Some statistics suggest that 30 to 40 percent of Hispanics are alienated from the Catholic Church and that some of these are joining other denominations.

Evangelical sects and groups are also exerting influence on Asian immigrants. At a recent conference in Denver, pastoral ministers from around the country told stories of Vietnamese, Cambodians, Chinese, Koreans, and other Asians who converted to Catholicism in their homeland but joined other churches when they arrived in the United States. This is largely due to the personalism and proactive evangelism of these churches.

Uninvolved Active Members

It is estimated that only 8 to 13 percent of the registered members of any given parish are *actively* involved in the parish's community life and ministry on a regular basis. Most parish members view the parish in terms of the church or the school. It is a *place*, not a community. In that place, they attend Mass and receive the sacraments, that is, they fulfill their religious obligations.

Through no fault of their own, these active yet uninvolved members do not receive the full benefit of their membership in the parish. They may not be experiencing the support, love, and challenge of this kind of faith community. In fact, this marginal membership may be responsible in part for some of the other forms of alienation already discussed. A recent letter to the editor of the *Chicago Catholic* lays some of the blame for this marginal membership at the feet of the parish.

> Dear Editor,
> Father Pat Brennan's approach to evangelization sees the unchurched and inactive Catholics as problems that can be solved. The way I see it, the Church is often the problem. If parishes—priests and people—

were really communicating the person and values of Jesus, then people would be flocking to church. But people do not want to be where clearly they are not wanted. What father would give his child a stone if he or she asked for bread?

As this letter points out, a person's perception of the Church is based on his or her experiences with the parish. If a person is made to feel unwanted or unneeded in the parish, then the Church becomes merely a cold and anonymous institution. For the Church to be a source of inspiration, the parish cannot chance giving out stones to its members. It must become a welcoming community in which *all* members are warmed and nourished by the person and word of Jesus Christ.

In an interview with a representative of the Alban Institute, Dr. Martin Marty had some interesting reflections to share about the uninvolved active member:

> One thing that we should have learned is that if you don't convert your own young and if you don't reach beyond your own, you might as well be celibate. Each generation [of Church] is going to be fewer and fewer. Not to evangelize is death. . . . I think that the mainstream church congregations just don't do enough with their collegiality, their conviviality, their community as an evangelizing agency. What I find, what every study of the unchurched finds, is that when you ask what would bring them back or bring them there for the first time, they don't say the prospect of better sermons or music or architecture or programs. They say, "If the people whose life-style I share, if the people I work with and hang out with find that something is important, I will entertain it. If everybody I know is doing aerobics, I might be invited by them, and then I'd do it. If everybody I know is jogging, and they invite me, then I might do it; and therefore if some of the church people who are important to me *invite me*, and I find meaning there, and there's a sacrality there, and there is a program of action there, and care there, I'd let it work on me and I'd become part of it. That's what I mean by saying you have to be inviting and you have to invite."

One of the stereotypes that Gallup and Castelli try to dispel in their book *The American Catholic People* is that large numbers of Catholics are leaving the Church. They find, rather, that large numbers of people are choosing to call themselves Catholic but are attending Mass less often. While there are many possible implications in this finding, there is one that is particularly disturbing. Has American individualism crept into the Catholic Church, eroding the centuries-old valuing of community and sacrament? Framed in another way, are more and more Catholics becoming merely "cultural Catholics," or "cultural Christians"?

The Church's evangelistic challenge is to invite everyone to kingdom living. That everyone includes active, inactive, and uninvolved Catholics, as well as the unchurched. Kingdom living includes ongoing personal transformation, discipleship, and community. Together, all are called to continue the mission of Jesus to the world.

2
A Reconciling Church

At a recent gathering of pastoral leaders in Chicago, William McCready spoke of his concerns as a Catholic sociologist. While there are as many or more Catholics now as there were twenty years ago, there has been a marked decrease in the number of people attending weekly Eucharist. Twenty years ago 75 percent of the American Catholic population attended weekly Mass. That figure is now around 45 percent. In addition, the last twenty years have not witnessed an increase in stewardship, or responsibility in financially supporting the local parish. More than 60 percent have not increased their donation over the past two decades. This financial inertia not only underscores a certain malaise among Catholics in supporting the Church but also flashes a red light of trouble ahead. How will the Church, and the local parishes in particular, be able to offer needed programs and services in the future?

McCready's research points to the emergence of two churches within American Catholicism: an inner circle of active believers, who are more involved in pastoral ministry than the laity has ever been before, and an outer circle of inactive and financially nonsupportive members, who still cling to some amorphous self-concept of being Catholic. In short, McCready warns that unless the Church begins to move in innovative ways to reach out to the outer circle, Catholicism will be the religion of far fewer Americans than the current 25 percent of the population. The Catholic Church *can* become a shrinking church on the American scene.

Professor Frederick Herzog of Duke University advocates a kind of twentieth-century reformation. "We need to stop putting Band-Aids on the big Church," Herzog wrote in a letter to me. "When will we become serious about the reformation of the Church through the small church, *koinonia?*" Herzog postulates that these church dilemmas are the same in both Roman Catholicism and Protestantism. His concerns were echoed in the December 22, 1986, issue of *Newsweek*, which described mainline Protestant churches as "sidelined." The article studied the mainline Protestant phenomenon of failing to pass on the faith to younger generations. Much of what was said about the growing number of alienated mainline Protestants could be said with equal accuracy about Roman Catholics.

What do we as Church have to offer someone who may be either unevangelized or alienated? Two realities stand out as both contemporary hungers and resources that we have to offer. The first is *community*. The second is *solidarity*.

COMMUNITY

Community is more than a crowd, or a loose association of people. Community speaks of people united in vision, goals, priorities, and life-style. Of course, not all communities are Christian communities. People form communities for a variety of purposes, from support around significant life issues to shared hobbies. Christian communities are unique because they are rooted in the person and values of Jesus. Their foundations are spiritual rather than just social, and their aim is to live the Gospel of Jesus in the world, or marketplace. Christian communities focus on sound catechesis that is relevant for an individual's unique life situation, while remaining connected and committed to the Church universal. Christian communities are inclusive and missionary in nature—never becoming cliquish and always being mindful of the reduplicative, inviting aspects of true discipleship. Christian community implies a kind of *intimacy*. The intimacy is not based on mutual self-gratification. Community members may not become best friends. But they do share life stories, life experiences, and prayer openly and honestly. And this sharing is filtered through the teachings and values of the Gospel.

The small, life-sharing, Gospel-focused groups (base communities) are becoming the most effective models of Church for the Catholic experience in Africa and Central America as well as for the Protestant evangelical experience around the world. Christian community is a kind of two-edged sword in terms of "marketing." In *Habits of the Heart,* Robert Bellah and others suggest that such Jesus-centered support groups are quite countercultural, juxtaposed to the independence and success orientation of most people in the United States. However, some sociologists estimate that somewhere around 25 percent of the American population are in some kind of small-community experience. As Dr. Marty indicated in an earlier quote, the need for community is at the essence of human nature. If the attracting community is not Gospel focused, it will have another magnet that appeals to sincerely experienced, heartfelt human needs.

I believe that the small-community explosion around the world is a reechoing of the experience of the early Christian churches, as well as paradigmatic of the Church in the future. Community is the best that we as Church have to offer the unchurched and alienated. In short, we must become more aware of the fact that we cannot invite people back to the same environment which may have caused their alienation in the first place. As Andrew Greeley and Mary Greeley Durkin state in the title of one of their books, we need to create *A Church to Come Home To.* We must become family. Leonardo Boff writes brilliantly in both *Church, Charism, and Power: Liberation Theology and the Institutional Church* and *Ecclesiogenesis: The Base Communities Reinvent the Church* that for centuries, the Church has presented too much and too often the "institutional model" as the primary motif or experience of Church. This model has little appeal to many people today. While there is a definite need for the institutional dimension of Church for purposes of creating unity and structure, it no longer is sufficient in attracting and nurturing believers. Nurturing can happen only in the environment of home, family, and community.

A Mexican priest once commented to me, "I don't know how you Americans can presume to evangelize people and help them grow in faith without some experience of genuine community." Frederick Herzog puts it another way: "In the large Sunday congregation, a person can remain anonymous. But in community, a member must be responsible and accountable to a small group of believers." Dr. John Hurston, with his daughter Karen, wrote a book entitled *Caught in the Web,* in which they document the growth of the Full Gospel Central Church in Seoul, Korea. In 1978 the church had 65,000 members, most of whom were in small communities. That number has now grown to over 500,000. Working with Dr. Paul Cho, Hurston came to see that all evangelization had to be geared toward the experience of community. After initial call and welcome—that is, primary evangelization—the people who respond to these efforts go on to become further evangelized through the experience of community. The Church in America needs to pray over and study new ways of being Church and of being parish—styles in which the active, inactive, and unchurched feel welcome, part of a family, part of a community.

Recognizing that evangelical Christianity has had to wrestle with its own demons and scandals, we also need to face and admit the obvious: The appeal of "tough discipleship" is growing. Why? On one hand, fundamentalism—whether in the form of Catholic doctrine or Scripture interpretation—has an attraction for those who seek a faith that does not admit of ambiguity, doubt, or struggle. Put more simply, religion can function to help people "put it on automatic." Whether expressed in ecclesial doctrine, magisterial pronouncements, or words from Scripture, "tough discipleship" seems to provide a person with an unerring map that leads to psychic and spiritual peace. Some people, however, are seeking "tough discipleship" in other forms and for other reasons. They are hungering for solidarity.

SOLIDARITY

Solidarity is much more than the unerring map that the various versions of fundamentalism provide. Solidarity is a felt experience of unity and oneness. The oneness is experienced in vision, values, relationships, and mission, or quest. This is what the term *solidarity* means. Real-life solidarity is seen in the struggle of the Solidarity movement in Poland. Polish Solidarity seeks human rights and justice in a governmental system that is authoritarian, autocratic, and lacking in respect for human dignity. Many people seeking community are searching for similar solidarity experiences. The atheism, agnosticism, and idolatry of Western culture are perhaps more muted than they are in Communist countries, but they are no less real. Searching, pilgrim people are seeking not "the map" of fundamentalism but rather groups that offer solidarity experiences—experiences that are truly countercultural. While the prophetic nature of many solidarity communities might further alienate some Christians, such communities are, on the other hand, what some estranged church members are looking for.

A PROCESS VIEW OF RECONCILIATION

In another book, *Guidelines for Contemporary Catholics: Penance and Reconciliation,* I develop in detail the historical evolution of the sacrament of Reconciliation, from its roots in Old Testament faith to contemporary practice. For the purposes of this study, I am focusing on one period in that long history—the second and third centuries. Baptism was experienced in the primitive Christian communities as a kind of *first penance,* or turning from sin and living a new life. The first Christians added to Baptism certain penitential practices that they inherited from the Jews to intensify the experience of conversion from sin and of reconciliation through God's love. The second century witnessed a great number of Christians denying their Christian identity to avoid persecution or death. The early communities were adaptable in meeting the needs of the first Christians. Thus, as some of these apostates presented themselves for readmission into the Church, local communities created a process of reconversion, quite similar to the process of the catechumenate through which non-Christians joined the Church.

In the third century, these processes took on a common style, or format, for reconciliation, or reconversion. Typically, the process of reconversion included the following:
- Confession of a sin to a bishop
- Exclusion from Eucharist
- A process of life reform that lasted up to several years
- Imposition of hands by the bishop, symbolizing the readmission of the candidate to the community and the Eucharist

The Order of Penitents

Some communities further ritualized the process of reconversion. In the ancient Order of Penitents, those who were just beginning their journey back to the Church were called *weepers*. Weepers had to stand outside the eucharistic gathering, obviously unworthy to enter. The next stage in the penitential process was the identity of the *kneeler*. Kneelers were allowed into the eucharistic gathering, but had to kneel in repentance in the back of the assembly. A third stage in the journey involved becoming a *stander*. This stage was close to celebrating full reconciliation with the community. The stander could stay for a portion of the Eucharistic Celebration, but had to indicate that he or she was a penitent by standing in an observable place.

The Catechumenate

The Order of Penitents parallels an even older process, that of the catechumenate, or what today is called the Rite of Christian Initiation of Adults. The catechumenate was a process for non-Christians to be socialized and immersed into the Christian community, assisted by the faith community and its ministers. This process of conversion often took several years. In the second and third centuries, the community was seen as the sacrament of the living presence of the Risen Lord. Beginning the Christian life, or reconciliation after sin or alienation, always was done in and through the community. The community was the sacrament of salvation and reconciliation. The catechumenate, especially in the third century, took on certain basic movements as paradigmatic for the journey of conversion. These movements were sequential, one leading to the next, as follows:
- A time for evangelization
- A time for catechesis or formation
- A time of spiritual purification (Lent)
- A time for commitment (the sacraments of initiation)
- A time for mystagogia, or a deepening of one's understanding and belief in the mysteries of salvation (as the new member found a place in the community)

Close scrutiny of the ancient Order of Penitents reveals that the process of reconciliation very much mirrored the model of the early catechumenate: evangelization, catechesis, purification, sacrament, and continued growth.

CONTEMPORARY RESTORATION

The experience of reconciliation as process had a number of values that need to be reappropriated for the contemporary Church. Confession of sin, genuine life change, true penance, deep contrition—all were done in the context of the community at Eucharist. Reconciliation with the community also gave the penitent a sacramental and existential experience of reconciliation with God.

Experiencing Reconciliation

While some Catholics, lay and cleric, are dismayed at the diminishing lines for confession and absolution, many pastoral ministers report that the hunger and thirst for reconciliation are profoundly alive in the hearts of faithful people. But the contemporary hunger for reconciliation seeks expressions and celebrations that transcend the impoverished, limited experience of reconciliation that many Catholics have known since the days of Trent. Catholics appreciate some of the many ways reconciliation is experienced in the parish:

- The penitential rites of each Eucharist
- Opportunities for both sacramental and nonsacramental communal celebrations of reconciliation
- Celebrations that employ general absolution where pastoral need dictates
- Profound experiences of healing and reconciliation in pastoral counseling and spiritual direction
- Down-to-earth, "I'm sorry—I forgive you" experiences in human relationships

All of the foregoing are examples of what can be called existential reconciliation. Existential reconciliation speaks of genuine life change—not just a return to what, who, and where people once were, but rather a rebirth to a new level of personal, relational, and spiritual oneness and integrity. The dynamic of reconciliation is not dead in the Church, as some would lament. Rather, reconciliation is simply seeking out and expressing itself in new forms, as it has in other centuries.

Remember, Return, and Rebirth

In recent years, some parishes have tried to adapt the Order of Penitents' process to their local needs and culture in order to facilitate the return of hurt, inactive, or alienated Catholics. In my own pastoral ministry, I came upon such a process inductively, or by bumping around in ministry, failing, learning, and trying again.

Over ten years ago, I began having hospitality evenings or weekends, at which people who had been away from the Church could come and tell their stories of hurt or alienation. Inactive members certainly need the catharsis, ventilation, and relational bonding that take place at these meetings, but they also need more. They need a process that is characterized by quality evangelization, catechesis, and healthy relationships with active church members. Many of the children of inactive members need catechesis and sacraments. So, my staff and I added an evangelization-catechetical series to our homecoming gatherings in several pilot sites, offering opportunities for family faith experiences.

Later, when study revealed that the time for reconciliation in the Order of Penitents was the Sacred Triduum, specifically at the Holy Thursday liturgy, we began to teach parishes to add a Lenten journey to their catechetical process, culminating with Holy Thursday, Good Friday, Holy Saturday, and the Profession of Faith with the catechumens at the Easter Vigil. Noticing the absence of returnees after they had completed this process, we later learned that what returnees need is not "Easter graduation" but rather continuing ministry and companionship after Easter, similar to the mystagogical period of the catechumenate.

Step by step, my staff and I developed a wholistic, integral process of return that mirrors the process of the Order of Penitents. Around the country now, a number of parishes are experimenting with such a process under a variety of titles, for example, "Remember and Return," "Returning Community," "Re-membering Church." After struggling with our own title, we decided to call our process "The Reconciling Community: Remember, Return, and Rebirth." We included the term *rebirth* in the title in order to emphasize that there is more to the process than just getting people back to church.

As I mentioned in the preface, sin, or alienation from God, is frequently described in Scripture as "forgetting" God or the values of Jesus and "wandering" either from the Lord or from the community. In the case of estrangement from the Church, it is true that individuals can forget and wander. But it is also true that the community can forget and wander from some of its members. True reconciliation involves both the alienated member and the alienating community. Each is called to remember and to return to the other. This process, however, does not result in a return to some past stance or relationship. If it is genuine, reconciliation results in a spiritual rebirth for the returning member and an atmosphere for conversion and reconversion of the faith community.

Saint John the Evangelist Parish, in a suburb of Chicago, is one of the parishes where my staff and I piloted and adapted this contemporary Order of Penitents. The process includes six stages: outreach and preevangelization, sharing of stories, commitment, purification, Easter celebration, and ongoing evangelization.

Outreach and Preevangelization. Spring months are used for extensive outreach by means of home visitation, newspaper ads, letters, and phone calls inviting people to become part of the reconciling community. The summer months are used for preevangelization, the beginning of reconciling relationships, and occasional social gatherings.

Sharing of Stories. The initial steps are followed up in the fall with meetings whose purpose is the sharing of stories of hurt and alienation. Wounds have to be lanced and returnees need to examine their roots and their reasons for becoming separated. This stage is a delicate one, requiring great sensitivity on the part of the team members.

While anger and hurt need to be released, and often there is healing in the release of these stories, some alienated members experience blockage and resistance at this stage. In effect, they do not want to let go of their anger. This is a curious but understandable reaction, which is also evident in counseling and psychotherapy. A client in therapy can gain insight into his or her problems, and can also see what needs to change if the problems are to be resolved. But often the client resists changing behavior. He or she is afraid of the new, perhaps more threatening life-style that lies ahead. Similarly, with alienated church members, holding on to anger keeps a person from seeking a new and sometimes threatening relationship with the community.

Commitment. After returning members are well into the process of evangelization, it is time for a question of commitment. The question becomes, "Who would like to continue in the process, with the intention of experiencing deeper healing and reconciliation, as well as new understanding of the faith tradition?" It has been the experience at Saint John's and other pilot sites that when an invitation to consider a deeper commitment to the process and the community is extended, the number of people involved in the journey begins to diminish. While the reconciling community should continue to try to maintain ties with those who choose to leave the process, ministers should realistically face the fact that the evangelization-catechesis process is an ever narrowing wedge. As the time for commitment or reconciliation comes closer, the people who are not ready will back away. Those who remain committed to the process continue sharing life stories. They also study and pray God's Word, focusing on the Sunday Scripture readings, and attend faith-formation sessions based on the Creed.

Purification. The Lenten season ought to be a special time of purification for returning Catholics. At Saint John the Evangelist, any member who wishes to do so may enter the Order of Penitents with the acceptance of ashes. The forty days of Lent are experienced as the sacrament of Reconciliation, in process. Ash Wednesday, or very early in the Lenten season, is the time for confession of sin and acceptance of God's mercy. The days of Lent are spent in prayer, fasting, and almsgiving. Each Sunday, ashes are put on again in place of signing oneself with holy water. The Holy Thursday evening celebration of the Lord's Supper includes individual absolution and imposition of hands, as well as washing away the ashes from the forehead of each penitent. (In this particular model, returning Catholics and others who have taken the Lenten journey are referred to as penitents. Other adaptations reserve the term *penitent* for those who are returning. This issue will be discussed in the next chapter.)

Holy Thursday is the time for the inactive and alienated to return to the Lord's Table. Father James J. Lopresti, S.J., of the North American Forum on the Catechumenate, has planned a beautiful ritual for returning penitents on Holy Thursday night. After absolution and imposition of hands, those who have been away and are returning stand around the altar with the celebrant. As the celebrant bows to kiss, or reverence, the altar, all of the returning members do the same. It is a powerful symbolic statement about returning to the Lord's Table. Newly reconciled members also are presented at and participate in the rest of the Triduum.

Easter Celebration. The Easter event ought to be a celebration of the entire community, including returnees, as they renew their baptismal vows and reclaim the meaning of their baptism. The journeys of the catechumens, the active members, and the returning members are different and yet the same: an ever-deepening immersion into the life, death, and resurrection of Jesus, an ever-deepening conversion.

Ongoing Evangelization. Returning members need attention and ministry after Easter, as neophytes do in the catechumenate process. At Saint John's, returning members meet regularly for worship and formation sessions. Participation in the various ministries of the parish will facilitate long-term nurture of the returning Catholics. Many parish ministries have built-in opportunities for faith sharing, growth, and skills development. Another opportunity is the small group, or base community, with its experiences of solidarity. In those parishes where the small group is becoming the basic experience of Church, folding returnees into small groups is a very effective means of ongoing evangelization.

3

Pastoral Issues

Anyone who is involved in the ministry of care and reconciliation has to deal with areas of human experience that may be uncomfortable and ambiguous. Some pastoral issues demand that the reconciliation process be continually shaped and adapted to reflect the changing understanding of both ministers and the community those ministers serve.

CALLING PEOPLE "PENITENTS"

One sensitive issue is the singling out of returning Catholics with the title and identity of penitents. I personally favor the idea that during the Lenten season, the entire community be invited to take on the identity of penitent. Other parishes around the country provide returnees and congregation alike with education geared to making them more comfortable with the presence in the parish of a subcommunity of returning Catholics.

Despite what a parish may call returnees, their visible presence in the community is of vital importance. Some parishes have been so concerned with not offending the returnees that their identity and presence is allowed to become blurred within the congregation as a whole. This is a disservice to the rest of the community. Just as a faith community is challenged to deeper conversion and growth by the visible presence of the catechumens at worship, so also the community can benefit by the visible presence and obvious identity of returning Catholics in its midst. For both catechumens and returnees, the faith community serves as a sacrament of God's presence and an instrument of conversion. In turn, the catechumens and returnees remind the whole community of the importance of conversion, reconversion, and reconciliation.

In short, ministers should not dull the impact that returning Catholics can have on the rest of the community. The returnees can help the parish grow as a reconciling community, and challenge it to think in ever new and fresh ways of other opportunities to be a reconciling, healing community.

DIVORCE, REMARRIAGE, ANNULMENT

Another highly sensitive issue with returning Catholics is the annulment process for divorced Catholics, especially those who have chosen to remarry outside of the Church and would like a second sacramental marriage. It is estimated that there are eight million divorced Catholics in the United States. Divorce and remarriage is no less a problem for Catholics than for the population at large. The number of cases being presented to marriage tribunals for annulments has increased over 8,000 percent since 1968, according to the North American Conference of Separated and Divorced Catholics. But even with this increase, the Canon Law Society of America estimates that only one-tenth of the potential returnees who could request an annulment are doing so. The other nine-tenths are not seeking annulment. Furthermore, a number of annulment cases are refused or are terminated because of uncooperative past or present spouses, or because they lack witnesses.

The Internal Forum

What does the reconciling community do with potential returnees who are resisting the annulment process or whose cases do not fit the process? The community is up against the pastoral issue of when, how, and whether to employ the internal forum, or "good faith" solution, to these sensitive situations. The internal forum is a process of conscience formation and moral discernment in which the facts, context, steps in reaching a decision, and the reasons for that moral decision are known to God, the person or persons involved, and a confessor or spiritual guide. The internal forum must be used only with great caution and discernment.

The principal area of concern is the danger of an erroneous public perception that it is quite acceptable for divorced and remarried Catholics to return to the Eucharist without going through an annulment of the first marriage. People who use the internal forum solution need to be aware that they could confuse or cause scandal to active members who do not understand the details of this solution. While there is no blueprint for avoiding scandal, couples who have had to use the internal forum solution may need to find a parish where there is no danger of scandal. The reconciliation of the divorced and remarried is further complicated by recent changes in the Code of Canon Law that do little to expedite or facilitate the process for those seeking an annulment. These changes, in most cases, result in making the process longer and more expensive—two factors that will undoubtedly make the process less attractive to those who are hesitant to begin with.

It is my pastoral opinion that respecting the external forum of the Church, returning Catholics ought to be encouraged to use the annulment process whenever possible. However, when that is impossible, or when personal conscience dictates otherwise, or when other pastoral situations arise (for example, when a non-Catholic spouse whose previous marriage needs an annulment is unwilling to submit to Catholic procedures), returning Catholics may need help and counsel regarding internal forum solutions. According to Father James Provost of the Canon Law Society of America, Catholics who are remarried without an annulment are not excommunicated but are in what he calls an "irregular" status (cf. *U.S. Catholic,* October 1984). Provost believes that an irregular status ought not to exclude a person from receiving the Eucharist if he or she in conscience believes that it is moral to do so. This is, then, a personal decision of conscience. In such a matter, a pastor or a spiritual adviser needs to show a great deal of spiritual sensitivity. The adviser can serve as a guide but should never impose his or her opinions. For example, the advisor should never say to the returning Catholic, "You ought to return to the Table of the Lord." The decision must be made by the person or persons in the irregular situation.

PERSONAL RELATIONSHIPS

The most important vehicles for the reconciliation of inactive members are personal relationships. Sociologist Dean Hoge, in his research for *Converts, Dropouts, and Returnees,* discovered that most returning Catholics in his control group cited a personal relationship as the determining factor in their return. According to Hoge, 55 percent were "family life" returnees. This term refers to people whose return to the Church was prompted by the desire to share in the religious education of their children or by the desire for religious unity in the family. Of those who returned, 8 percent reported being positively influenced by a spouse, 44 percent spoke of being influenced by relationships in general (including spouses, children, friends, relatives, or a priest), and 25 percent said a personal or family crisis facilitated a process of return.

The significant role of personal relationships in the process of reconciliation and evangelization should help define an approach to this ministry. The process of reaching out and inviting inactive members ought to proceed through the channels of *family ministry* and *family religious education.* The entire community should be sensitized to their responsibility to invite inactive neighbors and friends back to the community.

The Catholic Church is experiencing proselytizing, or "sheep stealing," by evangelical sects, cults, and groups like the Mormons and Jehovah's Witnesses. This proselytizing also points to the importance of relationships. Reverend John Blackoll, writing in 1984, reported over a million Hispanic Baptists living in Texas. He also mentioned that Hispanic membership in the Mormon Church had increased in the Houston area in the early 1980s by 150 percent. The Southern Baptist Convention now has over 1,500 Hispanic congregations, adding 150 per year. The Jehovah's Witnesses boast of 45,000 Hispanic members. Bishop Ricardo Ramirez of Las Cruces, New Mexico, predicts that the Catholic Church could lose 21 million members by the end of the century. In 1986, Archbishop Patrick Flores of San Antonio told the bishops of the United States of the extent of this proselytism. He reported that of 600 Polish refugees living in San Antonio, over 50 percent were being cared for by evangelical or mainline Protestant churches. In the Oakland, California, area, the Mormons reported the conversions of 800 Cambodians and 1,600 Vietnamese and Laotians from 1984 to 1986. The United Methodist Church recently set aside $7 million for outreach to racial and ethnic groups. In 1984, the Methodists claimed to have 360,000 blacks, 40,000 Asians, 40,000 Hispanics, and 18,000 Native Americans. Those numbers have certainly increased since then. In New York City, the Catholic Church lags significantly behind the Presbyterian Church (which is the most successful) and the Methodist Church (which is second) in attracting Koreans.

These successful proselytizing and evangelizing efforts are happening among the white middle class, Catholics and non-Catholics alike. What contributes to their success? A recent study by the Vatican on cults and sects—indeed any cursory analysis of most of evangelical methodology—reveals that the methods of these groups are largely a matter of personal relationships. Trained lay people reach out to people at every level of society and invite people into their homes and churches. Members also do extensive home visitation. They also carry their evangelical efforts to hospitals and institutions.

Public rallies and revivals provide quick, mass evangelization. Many such events also produce multilingual and multicultural outreach. As a follow-up, the evangelizers invite people to small faith-sharing communities. These communities, in turn, provide strategies for a rather simple, heartfelt spirituality. Also, they give new members quick access to active participation and leadership in a closed community of believers.

These evangelical communities are models of a strategy that somehow Catholics are loathe to employ. And yet, the Church cannot develop reconciling communities without a greater emphasis on *relationships* as the starting point for both the evangelizing and also the reconciliation process.

CYCLE OF EVANGELIZATION

The ministry of reconciliation needs to be viewed in the context of the bigger picture of evangelization. The reconciling community must be an evangelizing community. Without this evangelizing context, any efforts at reconciliation with the alienated will be ineffective and frustrating. The reconciling community needs to ask the question, "To what and to whom are we inviting people?" The process of *remembering, returning, and rebirth* needs to have meaning for both the community and the returnees. It needs to be a part of the continuing cycle of evangelization. This cycle includes nine elements, which grow out of a sense of mission for the reign of God.

1. Personal witness. The community raises the consciousness of each member on the importance of informal evangelization and efforts to reconcile alienated members.

2. Worship. The community experiences the centrality of the Eucharistic Celebration for evangelization, and the reconciling power of gathering and sharing God's Word and sacred food.

3. Faith-nurturing events. The community sponsors parish missions, revivals, cultural devotions, weekend retreats, marriage and family life enrichment experiences, and regional events.

4. Outreach. The community trains home-visitation teams to call on the inactive, alienated, and unchurched. These teams will also support the faith of active members, as well as reconcile with the inactives and the unchurched.

5. Catechumenal approach. The community develops ministries that parallel the RCIA and Order of Penitents—evangelization (awakening faith), catechesis (faith seeking understanding), purification (deepening discipleship), commitment or recommitment, follow-up ministries.

6. Enabled and empowered lay people. The community invites and educates its members to act as responsible leaders of various ministries. It discourages people from being satisfied to be "consumer parishioners" who expect the professional staff to provide all parish services.

7. Emmaus values and behaviors. The community espouses the values and actions of the Emmaus journey. The values include spiritual companionship, storytelling, questioning, and sharing meals and rituals. The parish experiences conversion and community in the context of these values and actions.

8. Small communities. The parish community directs its members to a network of small communities—each with a different identity, style, and focus, but all committed to prayer, faith sharing, caring for one another's needs, supporting one another, sharing Scripture and tradition, reaching out in ministry, and showing a spirit of inclusiveness.

9. A renewed vision of Church. The community emphasizes a vision of Church, or ecclesiology, based on the unity and equality of all believers in Christ. This vision recognizes the different gifts of the Spirit, or charisms, the Church needs to bring about the reign of God.

These nine elements may be diagramed as follows:

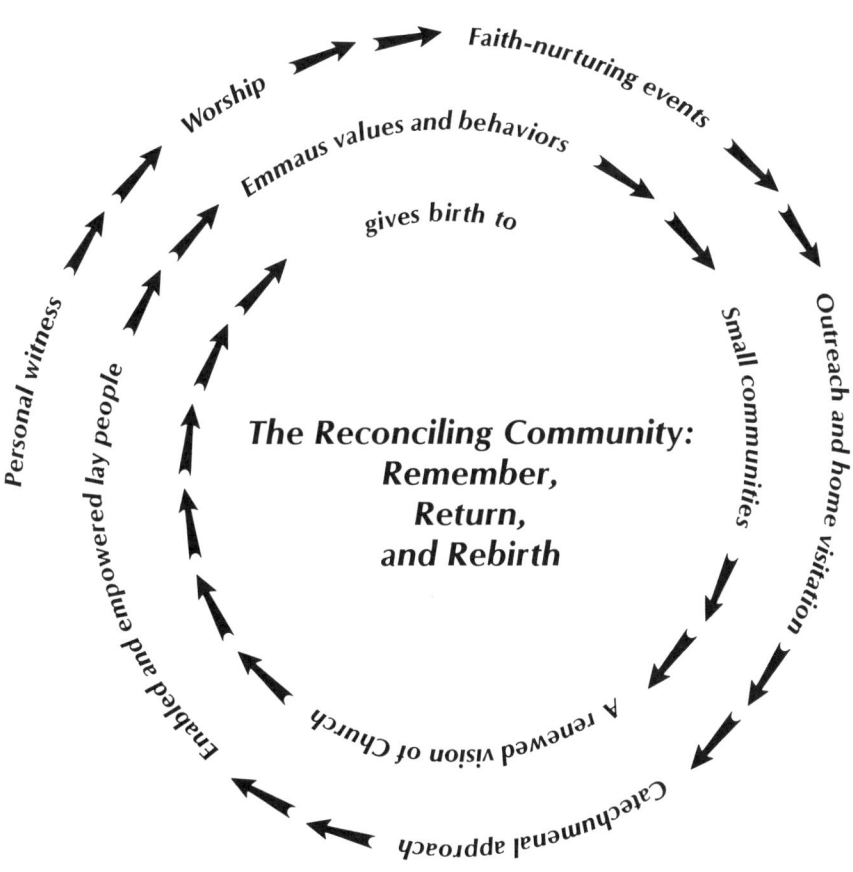

While not all these elements will be present to the same degree, all of them will have an important role to play in the reconciling parish. The ability to recognize and work with these elements is essential for anyone who wishes to minister in this kind of community.

4

Principles for a Ministry of Reconciliation

When I train parishioners for home visitation and for the re-member-return-rebirth process, I attempt to instill in them attitudes and principles that I feel are crucial for effective ministry. They form a kind of vision or discipline for this ministry. Some of the attitudes and principles that are discussed in this chapter are quite like those needed for working in the catechumenate.

TWO PARALLEL PROCESSES

It is important to note that there is a radical difference between catechumens (those seeking initiation into the Church) and those returning to the Church. Trying to mix returnees with those in the RCIA process can prove quite frustrating. The emotional tone of someone in the RCIA is quite different from that of someone in a process of return. Catechumens and those seeking full communion with the Catholic Church (for example, baptized Protestants) may be in the midst of life struggles associated with conversion, but they also usually display an excitement and enthusiasm about the Church. This is not always the case with many returnees. Quite frequently, there is a buildup of bad feelings, hurts, guilt, or any one of a number of negative emotions. This woundedness demands pastoral care and healing. Rather than being defensive, the reconciling community needs to develop the courage to ask questions about people's hurts or complaints, so that more and more of what is infecting their feelings and attitudes may be released. The negativity of some returnees can adversely affect the spirit of an RCIA community. Therefore, the thrust of this study is to offer separate but parallel processes for RCIA participants and returnees.

Manipulation

As a parish or a cluster of parishes begins to reach out to alienated and inactive members, two relational matters require monitoring. The first is manipulation. In the outreach stage as well as throughout the process of return, we as evangelizers do well to avoid anything that smacks of manipulation. Filling empty pews is not the goal of our efforts. Rather, our goal is existential reconciliation—a new oneness with self, others, and God. In outreach, indeed throughout the process, our posture needs to be one of nonmanipulative dialogue in which we encourage people to be reborn into the reconciling community and to return to the Lord's Table. Responses such as these, however, are by-products of loving, caring relationships.

Legalism

The other relational area that needs careful monitoring is legalism. This was touched on briefly in the chapter on pastoral issues. As pastoral ministers we need to tone down legalism in responding to people's hurts, alienation, and woundedness. We need to walk that slender tightrope of both respect for the magisterium and the external expectations of the Church, and the need that individuals have for personal, pastoral, healing responses to their pain. This is, then, a ministry of healing that offers both forgiveness and liberation.

SPECIFIC PRINCIPLES

Let us review some of the principles underlying the RCIA process to see which are especially helpful for reconciliation.

1. Conversion, or rebirth, involves time. No quick-fix program can effect reconciliation.

2. Reconciliation, like conversion, is a process, or journey. In emphasizing process over program, we are underscoring the movement of the Holy Spirit in conversion and rebirth. There is no programming the Holy Spirit.

3. In conversion and reconciliation, the best we can do is create an environment in which the Spirit may effect life change.

4. Reconciliation, in such a process motif, must be an adult- or family-centered experience. As discussed more fully in the next chapter, this adult-family orientation dramatically affects the way religious education, or catechesis, is done.

5. Reconciliation and conversion take place best in community. The small community becomes an instrument or context for life change for returnees. It also becomes a sign and a challenge to life change to the larger community, with whom it interacts. The larger community, in turn, is a sacrament for conversion for the small community.

6. The small reconciling community, nestled within the larger reconciling community, knows that everyone in the process—ministers and returnees alike—are in need of rebirth.

7. The process of reconciliation, like the catechumenal process, is a journey—a journey toward the Sacred Triduum, toward conversion and rebirth, toward vowing and revowing. The notion of vowing was a key factor in the early Christian community's understanding of *sacramentum,* or sacrament.

8. This reconciling process, with its Easter emphasis, is a deepening immersion into the life, death, and resurrection of Jesus.

9. Evangelization consists of those attitudes and ministerial actions that create an environment for conversion. A sign of conversion, or of reconversion (rebirth), is the beginning of a reconciled life.

10. The sacrament of Baptism and the sacrament of Reconciliation, a kind of "second baptism," must be joined to actual life change, rebirth, and conversion. Rituals must express reality. To celebrate sacraments without such changes of mind, soul, heart, and life-style is to render our sacred rituals powerless.

11. In both the catechumenal and reconciliation processes, the entire community is the minister of rebirth and conversion. However, in the name of the larger community, there emerges a small group of ministers who possess different gifts and charisms. These ministers provide a variety of services needed by both the initiated and the reconciled. Among these ministries are mentoring and companionship, catechesis, leadership in prayer and worship, and spiritual direction.

RITUAL AND STORY

Ritual, symbol, and liturgy are powerful tools in a process of reconciliation. Many pastors concentrating in the area of evangelization over the past years have discovered that evangelization needs to touch the imagination if it is to be effective. While knowing the doctrines and teachings of one's faith is important, *knowing* in a more personal, relational sense is at the heart of faith. James Loder notes well in *The Transforming Moment,* his analysis of spiritual transformation, that conversion is essentially a movement or leap of the imagination. Loder distinguishes between the *imaginary* and the *imagination*. The imaginary usually carries connotations of the "unreal," the "fabricated." The imagination, on the other hand, refers to that part of the human psyche or spirit that contains hopes, dreams, and values. The imagination is what prompts people to activity, what motivates them. This is why so much advertising appeals to the imagination rather than to the intellect. Advertisers know that it is the imagination that will move people to buy. Ancient cultures, like the one Jesus lived in, had an unarticulated appreciation of the imagination. Most of Jesus' evangelization was done through stories that touched the imagination.

Rituals and symbols perform in much the same way that stories do—they touch the imagination. In her study of young adult faith, *The Critical Years,* Sharon Parks retrieves the earliest meaning of the word *credo*. An intellectual meaning has traditionally been ascribed to the word *belief*. But *credo* originally meant "I give my heart to . . ." Evangelization that leads to conversion and reconciliation is about people's hearts, about helping them name what they have been giving their hearts to, and helping them move toward giving their hearts to the Lord Jesus.

In terms of the religious education of adults and young people, storytelling needs to be used more and more to touch hearts. Just as the stories of Scripture and tradition need to be told and retold, so returnees need to share their life stories. The reconciling community needs to help returnees tell their stories and also to help them name the God experience incarnate in them.

Related to imagination is *memory*. Memory is a special part of imagination that in a strong and unique way influences the present and the future. In working with returning Catholics, the reconciling community needs to have a special sensitivity to people's memories. Through storytelling, returnees will undoubtedly share memories of hurt and alienation. Ministers need to help returnees share the darkness of the past without allowing them to get "stuck" in it. Indeed, the purpose of the ministry of reconciliation is to companion people toward the light.

Whether stimulating the imagination in the present or healing memories of the past, symbol and ritual perform special functions. The root meaning of the word *symbol* is "catching something" or "things coming together." These connotations carry some of the same "movement" ideas that Loder spoke about in referring to the "leaping imagination." The symbols and rituals of both initiation and reconciliation help participants catch something, feel something, intuit something, leap to something. Ashes, oil, imposition of hands, scrutinies and exorcisms, the waters of Baptism, and the blessing of absolution—all of these symbols and rituals lift the imaginations of people and place them in special, out-of-the-ordinary time, in touch with mystery, in touch with the deepest part of themselves, in touch with the divine, and in touch with other persons in a formal and communal way.

5
Ministries of the Reconciling Community

In his lectures and writings, Father James Lopresti says we are not trying to get people to return to what they left or to "the way they were" before alienation set in. The process of the reconciling community ought to be a process of transformation, from which people emerge changed, different. Specifically, Lopresti says, a person emerging from such a process should come to the Lord's Table not as a passive spectator but as an apostle, a witness, and a prophet.

But this kind of dynamic reconciliation cannot take place in a human vacuum. So, the reconciling parish needs to have flesh-and-blood ministers who help the alienated member reenter an active community. There are many such ministries, but I would like to limit this discussion to three major categories: ministers of the Word, ministers of accompaniment (sponsors), and ministers of sanctification, prayer, and liturgy.

MINISTERS OF THE WORD

Much like the RCIA process, the process of reconciliation requires a number of ministers whose charism it is to bring the Word of God alive. Ministers of the Word include *evangelists,* who are comfortable sharing personal stories of how God has touched their lives; *catechists,* who are gifted in bringing the faith tradition alive; *lectors,* who proclaim the Word; *preachers,* who break open the Word of God and reveal what it meant in the past and what it means today; and *facilitators,* who spark and foster conversation and discussion.

These ministries are for all in the community, and they have to do with faith formation. But in the realm of faith formation, it is important to distinguish between pedagogy and andragogy. Pedagogy refers to learning methods and procedures used in educating children. Teaching children is usually influenced by several underlying principles:

- Children need input and content to store for use at a later time.
- The instructor knows the needs of the students.
- The curriculum is organized around prescribed needs.
- Learning often is equated with a rather passive absorption of information.
- Children have little experience to add to or to supplement the process of learning.
- Children must have readiness to learn subjects that are judged important by society, boards of education, and other authority figures.
- Evaluation of the learning experience is obtained through testing the students' understanding of the given material.

Andragogy, on the other hand, refers to the set of skills needed for educating adults. Andragogy operates out of different principles than those used in educating children:

- Adults prefer to learn things that have immediate usefulness in their lives.
- The educator helps adult learners name their needs and areas of interest.
- Learning proceeds best when education responds to perceived and articulated needs.
- Rather than passively absorbing information or being teacher dependent, adults learn best by interacting with others, sharing ideas and wisdom, and becoming self-directed in their learning.
- Adults have vast resources of experience that they can bring to the learning situation—experience that enriches both their learning and the learning of others.
- Educators ought not to presume readiness to learn on the part of adults; adults will be ready to learn if the educational effort responds to needs and interests.

- Evaluation of an adult learning experience is obtained through the reactions of the adults involved, as well as the influence that the whole experience has on the participants' lives.

Adult religious education raises other issues. Although adult religious education certainly has an intellectual component, perhaps the most important part of adult religious education is that which touches the imagination. In touching the imagination, education will influence values, and thus also behavior. Adult religious education at its best is sharing not just a "what" (content), but also a "why" (vision and values), a "how" (behaviors that flow from the vision and values), and, perhaps most fundamental, a "who" (a personal relationship with the Holy).

Adult learning is different from that of children because adults can make connections between the secular and the spiritual, while children often cannot. In other words, adults can discuss psychological issues, moral problems, the news, their relationships, intellectual matters, financial situations; and with help, they can connect all these subjects with their religious lives. The best adult religious education, then, begins with adult concerns. In doing faith formation with returning Catholics, the process must begin with their questions, needs, hurts, and resentments, and only later move to issues that the ministers feel to be important.

Effective Religious Education

Some good principles for the religious education of both children and adults are found in the work of Thomas Groome *(Christian Religious Education)* and James and Evelyn Whitehead *(Method in Ministry)*. For the sake of this discussion, the focus is on the relevance that these studies have for adult religious education. Groome sees religious education as essentially a political activity—a process of leading people. In addressing an issue in a religious education session, he suggests the following steps:

1. Help learners name their present position relative to the issue, as well as their feelings, thoughts, and questions.

2. Help learners explore *the why* of their position, probably by having them share past stories.

3. Share with learners a clear explanation of Scripture and tradition relative to the issue.

4. Facilitate dialogue among learners on how the Spirit is influencing them, and what is impressing them, as they pass through the first three steps.

5. Ask the political question: What should we do, as individuals or as a group, as a result of our sharing?

The Whiteheads' methodology is similar to Groome's. In their model of theological reflection, they suggest that issues be bounced against three poles in the process of reflection:

1. What does the dominant culture say?
2. What does Scripture say?
3. What does our tradition say?

This leads to the political question: What should we do?

Another person who has done some very important work on faith formation, or evangelizing catechesis, is Fritz Lobinger. Lobinger works at the Lumko Institute, an organization in South Africa that generates catechetical materials and trains lay people for pastoral ministry. He and his associates have developed a simple yet effective means of experiencing community and of sharing God's Word. They call it the "Look-Listen-Love" method. During the first step, Look, the participants share significant events that have occurred in their lives over the past week. Such sharing is based on the presumption that God is present in people's everyday experiences. During the Listen step, participants pause in silence to open their hearts and minds to the Holy Spirit. A question that each participant considers during the silence is "What is God saying to me in these everyday events that we have experienced and shared?" The second part of the Listen step is the proclamation of a Scripture passage followed by a discussion of what God may be saying to the group and to individuals through Scripture. During the third step, Love, the participants discuss how they can put into action the insights, values, and wisdom they have heard and shared.

A Simple Process

In working with returning Catholics, I have used a process similar to the one developed by the Lumko Institute. The methodology presumes that there is a theme for a given session. For example, suppose the theme of the session is redemption and what it means in our lives. The steps of the catechetical process look like this:

1. Journal entry. Participants jot down their thoughts or feelings on redemption. It should be stressed that there are no right or wrong answers. This step is intended to reveal to a person his or her present—the "what is" of his or her life regarding the topic.

2. Journal sharing. To the degree that participants are willing or able, they each share with another person or with the group the thoughts and feelings surfaced in the journal exercise. Pastoral ministers need to discern when sharing is best done one-on-one with a companion, in a small group, or in a large group.

3. Story relating theme to life. Someone from the ministry team tells a story of how redemption has happened or is happening in his or her life. This is a crucial step in which a doctrinal term like *redemption* is made real and understandable through the experience of the person sharing.

4. Dialogical talk. A catechist shares passages from Scripture as well as relevant Church teaching to shed light on the mystery of redemption. Afterward, the catechist invites comments and reactions from the group. Both the talk and the discussion should be focused, brief, and interspersed with relevant stories and personal examples.

5. Second journal entry. Participants write again on redemption, but this time they are to note any new insights they may have had since the beginning of the session.

6. Second journal sharing. Participants are invited to share what they have written with a companion, in a small group, or in a large group.

7. Prayer. To help participants internalize what they have learned, the session is concluded with an appropriate prayer. If possible, some simple symbolic actions may be added to the prayer.

Before going on, it is important to look for a moment at the basic assumptions of God's revelation as it affects the reconciling process. Avery Dulles, in his recent study *Models of*

Revelation, says traditional assumptions about God's revelation tend to limit it either to *history*—accounts of God's creative influence in the past—or to *doctrine*—churchy pronouncements that people must believe. Revelation, Dulles says, is rather a gradual awareness of God in individuals or groups. First, they notice the clues of God's presence and influence in their life journey. Then they interpret their lives and change because of the clues. Finally, they celebrate the clues and their own transformation in prayer and worship. The reconciling community sessions attempt to create an environment in which revelation as well as evangelization, reconciliation, and transformation may happen by the power of the Holy Spirit working in and through people.

How can participants be kept involved, motivated, and interested in these sessions? What will prompt them to continue coming? The key is to organize the sessions around the returning Catholics' agenda—their needs, hurts, questions, frustrations. Their agenda should be primary throughout the process, but especially in the initial sessions.

To help the participants work through the reconciliation process, I join two other resources to their personal agenda: the Creed and the *Lectionary.* So, each session consists of (1) discussing participants' hurts, issues, and questions; (2) studying and praying over elements of the Creed; and (3) studying and praying over the Sunday Scripture readings.

A priest attending a training institute with me expressed frustration that I was not sharing a quick-and-easy process which he could readily implement. I do not think that is how the reconciliation process works. It is messy, nonprogrammatic, and relational. Each community needs to develop its own process, constantly adjusting it to the needs of the individuals in the group. The only help I can give is to identify the ingredients and the skills needed for an effective reconciling community process.

MINISTERS OF ACCOMPANIMENT

While the sponsor, or companion, has a critical role in the RCIA ministry, he or she is perhaps even more important in the ministry of reconciliation. Not only must the sponsor develop a therapeutic relationship with the reconciling member, he or she must also help the returnee in the healing of wounds. As the reconciling community begins to gather together, some of those estranged from the Church will bear a great deal of hostility toward the Church, a parish, or some other church member. These people do not have the proper disposition for catechesis or faith formation. There is a need, therefore, to minister to them from two vantage points: preevangelization and evangelization.

Some Clarifications

Preevangelization is a ministerial and relational bonding with another person; it is entering the world of another person. In the case of the returning member, it is allowing that person to tell his or her story—specifically stories of hurt involving the Church. Intertwined with stories concerning the Church, there are inevitably other stories of personal struggles or sin: divorce, addictions, career crises, financial problems, parenting difficulties. Some of these stories may be discussed with the group; others may be privately shared with the sponsor. In such private sharing, the sponsor assumes the role of confidant.

At a national meeting on the reconciling community process, a group role-played different types of people who might seek reconciliation. One woman who was role-playing a sponsor confessed that she felt awkward about a particular situation. The person she was sponsoring had told her something extremely personal; it was not something that could be shared with the group. I told her that she was experiencing what many priests have gone through for years. Often, in one-on-one confession or in pastoral counseling, a priest hears stories of brokenness or sin that someone would not share in a group or community. As a result, only a person capable of confidentiality ought to perform such a ministry.

Once the reconciling member has dispelled his or her hostility through preevangelization, it is important to proceed to the evangelization stage. A clarification is needed here. Evangelization is not merely a stage that is preliminary to catechesis but also an attitude that must pervade the whole reconciliation process.

Michael Warren, writing in the March 1987 edition of *The Living Light,* is critical of scholars who equate the term *evangelization* with denominational affiliation. Evangelization, in the context of the reconciliation process, is not just about "getting people back to church." Rather, it is, to use Warren's term, *transformation*—both personal and communal. As hostility and woundedness fade, space is created in a person's heart to meet Jesus in a personal way—in a new, reborn way. Evangelization, then, is an attempt to move beyond hurt, sin, negativity, and anger. And the ministers attempt to create an environment in which community members are invited to embrace Jesus as Lord and Savior.

The Role of a Sponsor

The sponsor, or companion, plays a special role in evangelization. Sponsors and other ministers evangelize best when they give witness to their own healthy relationship with Jesus and to the nourishment that membership in the Body of Christ gives them. Warren speaks of this approach to evangelization in his excellent book *Youth and the Future of the Church*. Both preevangelization and evangelization often take place in simple, informal activities. These include participating in the discussions led by the ministers of the Word, making phone calls, inviting and driving reconciling members to community events or other parish gatherings, writing cards and letters, introducing reconciling members to other parishioners, encouraging and affirming reconciling members, informally praying with reconciling members, and serving as a liaison between reconciling members and the pastoral staff. Some parishes around the country ensure one-on-one sponsor-returnee time at each gathering of the reconciling community. During this time returnees can pray with their sponsor or share life stories and hurts they do not want to discuss in larger groups. Giving witness to this transforming relationship ought to be done at an appropriate point in the process, when and if it will be helpful for the members of the reconciling community. At all costs, it should be spontaneous. Scripted proselytism or spiritual one-upmanship should be avoided.

The following two letters were received by sponsors from returnees. The letters reveal the intense relationship that can develop between a sponsor and a returnee in the course of a reconciling community process.

> Dear [Sponsor],
> The last three days have really been a transforming experience for me—one that has opened a reservoir of strength that I can tap occasionally. I am writing to thank you for taking the time to listen to my woes

and to share with me some part of your own compassion and understanding. I am most deeply grateful. The sunlit stroll we took through the college grounds was really a turning point in my story, which seemed to be developing into a spiritual disaster. But now, because of your understanding and openness, I feel stronger.

Dear [Sponsor],
Last January, I came back to church after a very long time, looking for God knows what. I guess I've always needed spiritual guidance, but because of my divorce, I felt very alienated. When Father Gene told me about the reconciling community process, I knew it was for me. I must admit I was scared to go, but once I did, I immediately started to feel healed. Everyone was so supportive, especially you. You'll never know how much the program has helped during this really tough time in my life. You are an exceptional person, and the Bible you gave me was a special touch. I will cherish it always, and I will never forget your thoughtfulness and encouragement. Thanks so much for being there for me.

MINISTERS OF SANCTIFICATION, PRAYER, AND LITURGY

To pray with someone is to share faith with someone. Prayer is an immediate religious experience, or at least it can be. The genius of the catechumenal model of ministry is its integration of diverse ministries into a meaningful whole: Word, companioning, and prayer and religious experiences. Some ministers in the reconciling community process ought to serve as coordinators and leaders of prayer. This broad ministry includes the planning of prayer experiences at the regular sessions of the reconciling community, as well as the major rituals with the larger community at Eucharist. In most instances, leaders of prayer at the regular sessions ought to be parishioners. The major rituals at Eucharist are ordinarily led by a deacon, priest, or bishop.

At the regular sessions, it would be a good idea to expose reconciling members to as many styles of prayer as possible: formal, informal, structured, spontaneous, meditative, contemplative, conversational, silent, scriptural, writing in journals, singing and other music, prayer alone, and shared prayer. It should be remembered that reconciling Catholics may have left the church community with rather limited exposure to different styles of prayer. Therefore, respectful patience ought to be the attitude of the ministers in introducing or reintroducing returning members to various styles of prayer.

In praying with reconciling Catholics and in modeling prayer styles, ministers need to keep in mind that they err, evangelically and spiritually, when they take a "cookie-cutter" approach to ministry. Such an approach presupposes that everyone in a given process or program will turn out the same, that conversion will "look" the same in all people. As Adrian van Kaam has pointed out in his work on spiritual direction, and as James Fowler and Sharon Parks have shown in their work on adult vocation, God is calling each person to a unique direction, a unique style of partnership.

Parks and Fowler, as well as Allan Bloom in his best-seller *The Closing of the American Mind*, all speak of the dysfunctional aspects of dominant culture in the West today. Fowler speaks of the vocational mind-set in America as the pursuit of "my destiny." Parks writes of dominant culture as a mentoring force, and the foundation or goal of the mentoring as "the wallet." Bloom sees in the "openness" of contemporary culture a closing of the mind, spirit, or soul—an insensitivity to the depths of what it means to be human.

Ministers of sanctification—working with ministers of the Word and ministers of accompaniment—seek to facilitate the process of reconciliation by transcending the "my destiny," "wallet" oriented, "dead within" aspects of dominant culture. In praying with reconciling members, sharing stories, and discussing matters of the Spirit, ministers of sanctification try to help people hear their own calling to partnership with God, find their own spiritual direction, experience their own spiritual awakenings, and discover the spiritual discipline that is most congruent with each person's personality and temperament. (Some exploration of this latter dimension has been done by Chester P. Michael and Marie C. Norrisey in *Prayer and Temperament: Different Prayer Forms for Different Personality Types* and by David Keirsey and Marilyn Bates in *Please Understand Me: An Essay on Temperament Styles.*)

The prayers of the reconciling community are not just "prayer alone" experiences. The reconciliation process is marked by regular liturgical moments, or rituals, in the eucharistic assembly. These rituals mirror similar peak moments in the catechumenal process. As for catechumens, so also for penitents or returnees, the process of conversion or reconciliation, along with the liturgical rituals, should be explained to the entire congregation before the fact and during the process.

6

Synthesis

At this point, it is a good idea to synthesize and organize what has been discussed thus far about the reconciling community process. In addition to summarizing the steps of the process and detailing some possible liturgical moments that are appropriate for the reconciliation process, this chapter demonstrates how these steps can be used in slightly different ways, in different contexts, with the same net results—reconciliation with the alienated, the hurt, or the inactive. Two adaptations of the process are presented: (1) a process for the welcoming and integration of newcomers into the parish and (2) a process approach to all parish-based sacramental preparation. It is my belief that while the reconciling community will touch some people in need of reconciliation, welcoming newcomers and working with families in sacramental preparation can also create opportunities for evangelization and reconciliation.

THE RECONCILING COMMUNITY PROCESS

As you study the following overview of the reconciling community, remember that all such outlines and schemas are only approximations of what may take place in the process. They are guidelines, not recipes, for evangelization, reconciliation, and conversion work. What is not seen or sensed in the overview is the human struggle, the life stories, the searching, the heartache, and the healing and joy that people taking the journey experience.

STEP ONE: EVANGELIZATION PERIOD

- Reaching out via home visits, letters, newspaper ads, media, and each-one/reach-one efforts
- Informal gatherings for storytelling—sharing of questions, hurts, and needs
- Relational bonding
- Social gatherings

Discernment—decision to continue

STEP TWO: FORMATION PERIOD
(Catechesis)

- Rite of entrance
- Regular gatherings
- Andragogy: addressing the needs of adult learners, practical application of faith in daily life
- Three resources for catechesis: participants' questions and needs, the Creed, and the *Lectionary*
- Liturgical moments: presentation of the Scriptures, minor exorcisms, blessing of the penitents, anointing
- Optional: liturgical dismissal of those in the process of reconciliation

Discernment—decision to continue

STEP THREE: LENTEN PENITENTIAL SEASON

- Whole community, including those in the reconciling community process, begins sacrament of Reconciliation and enters the Order of Penitents—confession of sin, request for God's mercy, a penance chosen for forty days
- Liturgical moments: scrutinies, presentation of the Creed and the Lord's Prayer
- Optional: dismissal of those in the process of reconciliation-return
- Members of the congregation sign their foreheads with ashes each Sunday during Lent

STEP FOUR: HOLY THURSDAY CELEBRATION

- Welcoming of the reconciled at beginning of Eucharist
- Ritual of returning to the Lord's Table
- Individual absolution of the reconciled, sharing the sign of peace, and wiping off the ashes
- Veneration of the altar
- Eucharist for Holy Thursday continues

STEP FIVE: FOLLOW-UP

- Ministries that help returning Catholics find a place
- Rebirth *in* the reconciling community
- Rebirth *of* the reconciling community

Before moving on, let's discuss further three of the items listed above: the evangelization period (step one), discernment, and the follow-up (step five). The essence of evangelization is the proclamation of the person and lordship of Jesus, leading people consciously to embrace Jesus as Lord. But before such a dialogue of conversion can occur, significant time often needs to be spent in preevangelization. Preevangelization refers to the forming of relationships, the beginning generation of community, and, perhaps most important, the lancing of anger, disdain, or alienation that may exist between an individual and the Church, religion, or God. Unless preevangelization and evangelization are done well, the ensuing stages will not be effective.

Traditional discernment of spirits is an important part of the reconciliation process. This discernment is not an individual search, however. The proper context for discernment is within the reconciling community. Only in community can the returning Catholic test the genuineness of his or her return. The sponsors provide the link to the whole community as they help the returning Catholic with the discernment process.

Another term used to describe the follow-up period is *mystagogical gathering*. After Holy Thursday, it is important for the reconciling community to gather regularly, both at Sunday Eucharist and for formation and support sessions. In other words, Holy Thursday must not be experienced as graduation. Rather, the time after Holy Thursday ought to be used for recapitulation of the whole process, for life planning, and for discernment as to how returning members will integrate into the community and how they will minister in the parish or work place.

SAMPLE SERVICES

The following sample services show some possible liturgical moments that are appropriate for the reconciliation process.

Rite of Entrance

This service signals the beginning of step two in the reconciling community process—the formation period. Some parishes around the country perform this ritual privately since the returnees often have not developed sufficient trust to allow them to appear publicly as a community at a large gathering. Other parishes, however, perform the ritual in the context of a weekend liturgy.

Opening Song: "Hosea"

Presider: We are here because of our concern for the hurt and alienation in our community. We do not seek merely to persuade people to come to church. Rather, we want to be a reconciling community. We want to remember the people we have forgotten or screened out; we want to return to people we have wandered from. We pray also that they will remember the Body of Christ and return to their spiritual home. As the initiation of new members breathes new life into the Church of God, we are convinced that reconciliation with our brothers and sisters will bring rebirth for them and for us. Let us seek the remembering, the returning, the rebirth of true reconciliation. To be a reconciling community for others, we must also be in a constant stance of reconciliation ourselves. So, tonight, as we prepare for the ministry of reconciliation, let us confess our own need for healing, our own sin, and the great power of God's love.

Let us pray. Father, we are convinced of your graciousness, your goodness, and your love. We confess your great mercy. We lift up to you our troubled spirits, our broken relationships, our anxieties and fears, our doubts and discouragement, our obvious and our subtle sin. Heal the brokenness in us; forgive and cast out the sin and evil in us. As we grow in reconciliation, help us become ambassadors of reconciliation for others. We ask this through Christ our Lord.

Assembly: Amen.

God's Word: Psalm 51:1–19

Song: "Dwelling Place"

God's Word: Mark 9:14–29

Homily

Presider: Why have you come here today?

Assembly: To be reconciled and to become reconcilers.

Presider: What is this reconciliation that you seek?

Assembly: It is the sign that we are living converting lives.

Presider: Father of love and mercy, I thank you in the name of my brothers and sisters, for we have experienced your guiding presence in our lives. Today in community we answer your call to reconciliation. We praise and bless you, Lord.

Assembly: We praise and bless you, Lord.

Presider: As a sign that we are sponsoring and companioning one another on this journey of reconciliation, I ask each sponsor to place your arm around the shoulder of the person you are sponsoring. I ask you—ministers and community—are you in need of healing?

Assembly: We are.

Presider: We have all come here to enrich ourselves in the wisdom of Jesus and his spirit of reconciliation. Indeed, we want to become ministers of reconciliation that we might better do this. Let us lay aside the demons and idols that keep us from the Lord, from one another, and from becoming what God calls us to become.

(The presider invites the assembly to respond "Free us, O Lord" after each invocation.)

Presider: From all anxiety, . . .
From all discouragement, . . .
From physical, psychological, and spiritual wounds, . . .
From the illusions of the world, . . .
From sin, . . .
From physical and spiritual poverty and hunger, . . .
From grief, . . .
From resentment and grudges, . . .
From materialism, . . .
From racism, . . .
From sexism, . . .
From militarism, . . .
From cruelty and injustice in our own Church, . . .

I ask you to get in touch with your hurt, woundedness, or sin. I invite any and all of you to ask for God's healing, either publicly or in the quiet of your hearts.

(Silence)

Our God—Father, Son, and Spirit—we renounce these and all the demonic forces that keep us from kingdom living. Multiply our efforts at conversion and reconciliation through the power of your Holy Spirit. We ask this through Christ our Lord.

Assembly: Amen.

Presider: My sisters and brothers, the cross is the sign of our faith. It speaks of the great sacrificial love of Jesus and his passover to the Father in which we share through Baptism and Reconciliation. As we begin this process, let us recommit ourselves to Jesus and the mystery of the cross.

(The presider invites the community to engage in a ritual of signing themselves with the cross. As the presider mentions each part of the body, the sponsor should make the sign of the cross on the community member he or she is caring for.)

Presider: Receive the sign of the cross on your forehead. May you think and feel as Jesus did.

Receive the sign of the cross on your eyes. May you see with the eyes of Jesus.

Receive the sign of the cross on your lips. May you speak only as Jesus would.

Receive the sign of the cross in your heart. Let your heart be his tabernacle.

Receive the sign of the cross on your feet. How happy are the feet that bring good news to the poor.

Let us pray. We embrace your cross, Lord. Lead us through the mystery of the cross to the victory of the resurrection. We ask this through Christ our Lord.

Assembly: Amen.

Presider: As you go now to experience the rest of your journey, may the Lord bless and keep you. May the Lord let his face shine upon you and be gracious to you. May the Lord look upon you and give you his peace.

Assembly: Amen.

Closing Song: "In Him We Live"

Ash Wednesday

The beginning of Lent is the perfect day to invite both active members and returnees to participate in a process of penance—to become, in fact, "penitents." The following rite of entrance into the Order of Penitents can take place at the major Ash Wednesday liturgy, and it signals the beginning of step three in the reconciling process. *(Note:* Although a private confession of sin takes place at the service, those who have entered the Order of Penitents are encouraged to celebrate individual confession sometime during the forty days of Lent.)

(Position in the liturgy: After the opening prayer and Liturgy of the Word, the presider addresses the active and returning members who have decided to become "penitents.")

Presider: Why have you come here today?

Penitents: To spend these forty days with Jesus in a spirit of fasting, prayer, and works of charity.

Presider: And what will Jesus bring to your lives?

Penitents: He will bring us both healing and challenge.

Presider: This Lent is a journey, a passover for all of us. Let us confess God's great love and also our own woundedness and sin, our need for healing. Let this Lenten journey be a journey to resurrection and new life for all of us; and for our returning brothers and sisters, let it be a journey back to the Table of the Lord.

(The presider calls each penitent to kneel and, facing the cross, to name quietly the sin or the hurt in his or her life that needs healing. After all the penitents have had a chance to express their sorrow, the presider blesses the ashes.)

Presider: Lord, bless these ashes by which we are reminded that we are dust. Pardon our sins and keep us faithful to prayer, fasting, penance, and the conviction of your love for us.

(The presider then addresses the penitents.)

Remember that you are dust and to dust you shall return. I invite you to come forward to receive ashes. You have confessed your need for healing and for forgiveness. Accept the ashes as an invitation to return to God.

After receiving your ashes, step to the side and decide what your Lenten penance will be. In what ways will you try to turn your life around? In what ways do you need to cooperate more with God?

(The penitents are signed with ashes and quietly name their penance before the cross.)

Presider: I now invite the rest of the congregation to come forward to receive ashes, a reminder of our mutuality and God's victory over brokenness.

(After everyone has received ashes, the presider concludes with this prayer.)

Presider: God our Father, you will all to be saved and to come to the knowledge of your truth. Send workers into your great harvest that the Gospel may be preached to every creature, and your people, gathered together by the Word of life and strengthened by the power of the sacraments, may advance in the way of salvation and love. We ask this through our Lord Jesus Christ, your Son, who lives and reigns with you and the Holy Spirit, one God forever and ever.

Assembly: Amen.

Holy Thursday

Following the ancient tradition of the Church, the parish community can welcome and reconcile returning members at the Holy Thursday celebration. As they do on each Sunday of Lent, those who come to Eucharist sign themselves with ashes as they enter church. The community has been well informed and educated throughout Lent about this process approach to reconciliation, and how it reaches a climax on Holy Thursday night. *(Note:* As part of the reconciliation celebration, some parishes may also want to include the washing of the feet, with the newly reconciled washing the feet of the community members, or having their own feet washed. By extending the identity of penitents and the opportunity for reconciliation to the entire community, any hint of an indicting attitude that might be perceived by the returnees is erased.)

(Before the Eucharist, the celebrant walks in silence with the other ministers to the vestibule, or narthex, of the church. He greets the reconciling members who are waiting there. Gathering outside the body of the church makes an important public statement. If possible, the doors between the vestibule and the church should be closed. However, the assembly inside the church should be able to hear what is going on. If they are deaf to the proceedings, the symbolic power is lost. After an informal greeting, the celebrant faces the reconciling members

and their sponsors. The dialogue below can serve as a model. It would be ideal if the celebrant would tailor the dialogue to the specifics of the local parish and the people in the process.)

Celebrant: We celebrate tonight the beginning of the three most sacred days of the year, the Sacred Triduum. Tonight focuses on the beginning of our Lord's paschal journey. Let us begin this passage of reconciliation and new life. Holy Thursday draws our attention to two important realities. This night emphasizes the great gift of the Eucharist, which we share at the Lord's Table. And on this night a community of people who have engaged in a journey of reconciliation complete that process by returning to the Table of the Lord.

(The sponsors now stand next to the reconciled. Each sponsor extends an arm around the shoulders of the person he or she is sponsoring.)

Celebrant: I ask the sponsors here tonight: Do you feel that our brothers and sisters have fasted, prayed, done penance, and reconciled with self, others, and God, so that they can fittingly approach the Lord's Table?

Sponsors: They have.

Celebrant *(to the reconciled):* You who have taken this journey of reconciliation, do you seek to complete the journey by taking your place at the Lord's Table?

The Reconciled: We do.

Celebrant: I open the doors of the church to you. With your sponsors, follow me to the Table of the Lord.

(At those words, the choir and the congregation can begin a rousing entrance song appropriate for Holy Thursday and for this ceremony. The reconciled and their sponsors immediately precede the celebrant in the procession to the altar. The reconciled gather in front of the altar and wait there. The celebrant goes at once to the presider's chair. After the entrance song is finished, the celebrant leads the whole congregation in one of the penitential rites from the Sacramentary. When the rite is finished, the celebrant steps down, faces the reconciled, and prays the following.)

Celebrant: Father, through your powerful grace, heal, forgive, and reconcile these your servants, who have confessed their sin, confessed your love, and prayed and done penance so as to be restored to communion with the Church and with you. We praise you and thank you for leading them and guiding them back to our family table. We pray through Christ our Lord.

Assembly: Amen.

(The celebrant now extends his hands over the small reconciling community.)

Celebrant: God, the Father of mercies, through the death and resurrection of his Son, has reconciled the world to himself and sent the Holy Spirit among us for the forgiveness of sins. Through the ministry of the Church, may God give you pardon and peace.

(Then the reconciled step forward for individual absolution. Laying hands on each person, the celebrant continues.)

Celebrant: I absolve you from your sins in the name of the Father, and of the Son, and of the Holy Spirit.

(The celebrant shares the sign of peace with each of the reconciled. Another minister then wipes the ashes from the forehead of each person. All of the reconciled then take places at the altar, facing the congregation. When all have gathered there—including the celebrant—they bow and kiss, or reverence, the altar. If a number of priests are available, other people in the congregation can come forward to receive absolution and have the ashes wiped from their foreheads. If time permits, each person receiving absolution can also kiss the altar. This public gesture can be a very powerful experience for the whole congregation. When everyone requesting absolution has received it, the whole congregation sings the Glory to God. During the singing, the reconciled group is seated in places of honor near the front of the church. The Eucharist for Holy Thursday continues from this point.)

Other Reconciliation Opportunities

Anointings. As in the catechumenate, an anointing with oil can take place at any time during the process, when the community feels prayers and rituals for strength are needed. Most often, these would be done outside the eucharistic assembly. (Guidelines for adapting the RCIA rituals for the reconciling community are given in the Appendix.)

Presentation of the Scriptures. At Eucharist or in the context of a small group, returnees can be presented with the book of Scriptures, or if they prefer, have their own Bibles blessed, consecrated, or enthroned. It is best that such a ritual be done early in the process, since the Scriptures are foundational throughout the process.

Handing on of the Creed and the Lord's Prayer. During the third week of Lent, or the week of the first scrutiny, the congregation prayerfully recites the Profession of Faith, or Creed, thus handing on to the catechumens the ancient credal statement. During the fifth week of Lent, or the week of the third scrutiny, the congregation hands on the model prayer, the Lord's Prayer. While the actual rite suggests that these rituals be done during the week, I always do them at a weekend liturgy for the benefit of both the catechumens and the assembly.

For those engaged in a reconciling community process, these two beautiful rituals could be adapted and done at another Eucharist, distinct from the one being used for catechumens. The rituals should be designed to speak to those who are returning to the Body of Christ rather than joining it for the first time. (Guidelines for adapting the RCIA rituals are given in the Appendix.)

The Scrutinies and Exorcisms. The scrutinies are prayers of petition that invite candidates to listen to and penetrate their own hearts in order to discern whether they are working on purifying their minds and hearts. Exorcisms are essentially prayers of healing, pronounced over candidates, that the Spirit of God will free them from sin and brokenness. The scrutinies and exorcisms are done on the third, fourth, and fifth Sundays of Lent.

Reconciling community leaders need to decide whether they will adapt some of the scrutinies and exorcisms for their reconciling process. As I mentioned before, these adaptations should be used at a liturgy distinct from the catechumens' gathering. (Guidelines for adapting the RCIA rituals are given in the Appendix.)

Dismissals. The ministering team or community needs to discern whether dismissing the penitents or returnees is pastorally wise. Dismissals are effective in causing both those being dismissed and those remaining in church to reflect on the meaning of staying at the Lord's Table and celebrating the full meal. Since most in the reconciliation process will not be taking Eucharist until Holy Thursday, it seems appropriate to use dismissals. If it becomes a pastorally explosive situation, then they need not be used. Both returnees and catechumens develop a better feeling about dismissals if being dismissed is explained as their ministry to the rest of the congregation; that is, it causes the congregation to reflect on the meaning of the Eucharist in their own lives.

PROCESS FOR WELCOMING NEW MEMBERS

Many people's first encounter with a new parish takes place when they go to register at the rectory or the parish office. The typical registration is handled by a secretary, a volunteer, or an administrative assistant. The procedure usually is a polite but rather cold welcome into a faith community. To help people understand the true meaning of parish membership, some Catholic and Protestant churches around the country are experimenting with a welcoming process which parallels that of the catechumenate and the reconciling community. Such a process not only supports newcomers who have an active faith life but also provides an opportunity for encouraging those who have been inactive—or even alienated from the Church. To put the process outlined below into action, a parish needs the help of a variety of ministers and the cooperation of the whole faith community.

STEP ONE: OUTREACH

- Initial contact can be done in one of two ways: (1) newcomers contact the parish, and a neighborhood minister is notified to visit them, or (2) a neighborhood minister stays up-to-date on people who have moved into the area, and drops by to welcome them.
- The pastor or a pastoral staff member phones or writes a letter to the newcomers.

STEP TWO: RITE OF INTRODUCTION

- During a weekend Eucharist, the newcomers are introduced to the faith community in a special ceremony.
- The times when the ceremony will take place should be rotated so that everyone in the community has a chance to participate in the process.

STEP THREE: FORMATION

- The newcomers are invited to several small-group, faith-sharing experiences, which are led by trained ministers.
- Some of the topics that can be discussed at these meetings are the parish mission statement, the vision of the community, ministry and the ministries available in the parish, personal and familial spirituality (prayer, worship, justice), and the meaning of active parish membership.
- Neighborhood ministers or sponsors call on the newcomers regularly.
- The names of those joining the community are published in the parish bulletin.

STEP FOUR: RITE OF COMMITMENT

- At a weekend Eucharist, the newcomers recite the parish mission statement as a sign of covenanting with the parish.
- The celebrant and the faith community perform a ritual of welcome.

STEP FIVE: FOLLOW-UP

- Sponsors or neighborhood ministers help the new members get involved in parish groups, ministries, or programs.

The parishes that are using such a process to welcome new members have decided on this course of action because it has been their experience that many people who register in the parish quickly recede into inactivity or maintain mere liturgical contact with the parish. Also, such a process, which targets both active and inactive types, could actually stop an alienation syndrome or pattern before it begins.

There is also an educative component to the welcoming process. The essential message of the process is that membership in a parish includes more than just placing one's name on a list. It means taking on responsibilities, changing some behavior patterns, and assuming a new identity. A newcomer process that is equivalent to a covenanting process with the Body of Christ gives true meaning to registration in a parish.

SACRAMENTAL PREPARATION PROCESSES

The pastoral pragmatist in me sees sacramental preparation as perhaps the most opportune time for evangelization and reconciliation with the alienated or inactive. Many alienated Catholics still value religious education and sacramental preparation for their children. The children, and their sacramental steps, then become opportunities to evangelize the entire family, and specifically to reconcile with alienated parents. It should be made clear at this point that in any of the processes discussed in this chapter, those who minister in such processes do not bring about conversion or reconciliation. At best, they create an environment or atmosphere that is conducive to conversion or reconciliation.

During sacramental preparation, there are five stages to which a parish can add a "conversion process motif."

1. Evangelization. In this early stage, relationships are formed and the participants' needs and questions are addressed. Formal catechesis is reserved for later in the process.

2. Catechesis. This stage ought to begin with a formal rite of beginning, or entrance (as an individual, couple, or family), performed at a weekend liturgy. The catechetical period should cover topics that speak to the faith and life needs of the individuals, parents, or families. Catechesis presumes total community involvement, including family worship. Many parishes, to accomplish the latter, conduct family catechetical sessions connected with one of the weekend liturgies.

3. Proximate preparation. This stage of sacramental preparation includes another liturgical experience with the Sunday assembly, as well as the equivalent of what catechumens experience in the Lenten purification.

4. Celebration of the sacrament. Whatever the sacrament, it ought to retrieve and celebrate the ancient notion of *sacramentum* as vow or life change. Each sacrament, in fact, is a reavowing to the essential meaning of the original vow of Baptism.

5. Postcelebration ministries. Through a variety of ministries, programs, and follow-up efforts, the parish ought to strive to ensure that the sacramental moment is not viewed as a graduation ceremony, but rather that it is seen as a new beginning within the faith community, a new relationship with the Lord, and a new sense of mission.

The following charts show how these five stages can be used with Baptism, first Eucharist, first Reconciliation, Confirmation, and Marriage.

BAPTISM
(Parents and Sponsors)

1. Evangelization
   - Home visits by neighborhood ministers
   - General inquiry sessions, tending to participants' needs and questions
2. Catechesis
   - Rite of beginning
   - Topics to be covered: parents' faith history, responsible parenting, meaning of Baptism, Christian responsibility, role of parents and sponsors
3. Proximate Preparation
   - Sessions with celebrant
4. Celebration of the Sacrament

5. Postcelebration Ministries
   - Small communities
   - Sponsor or neighborhood ministry follow-up
   - Support programs on marriage and parenting
   - Adult education
   - Retreats

FIRST EUCHARIST
(Candidates and Parents)

1. Evangelization
   - Home visits
   - General inquiry sessions

2. Catechesis
   - Rite of beginning
   - Topics to be covered: family faith, Jesus—the Bread of Life, eating the Bread of Life, meal and sacrifice

3. Proximate Preparation
   - The parish Lenten retreat
   - Ritual at weekend Eucharist beginning final stage

4. Celebration of the Sacrament

5. Postcelebration Ministries
   - Small communities
   - Sponsor or neighborhood ministry follow-up
   - Support programs on marriage and parenting
   - Adult education
   - Retreats

FIRST RECONCILIATION
(Candidates, Sponsors, and Parents)

1. Evangelization
   - Home visits
   - General inquiry sessions
2. Catechesis
   - Rite of beginning
   - Topics to be covered: family faith, God's love and forgiveness, sin, reconciliation in the home and in relationships
3. Proximate Preparation
   - The parish Lenten retreat
   - Ritual of beginning final stage
4. Celebration of the Sacrament
5. Postcelebration Ministries
   - Small communities
   - Sponsor or neighborhood ministry follow-up
   - Support programs on marriage and parenting
   - Adult education
   - Retreats

CONFIRMATION
(Candidates, Sponsors, and Parents)

1. Evangelization
   - Visits with staff members
   - Involvement in youth ministry programs
2. Catechesis
   - Rite of beginning
   - Topics to be covered: Meaning of vow, completion of initiation, Christian responsibility, promise of the Spirit, witnessing

3. Proximate Preparation
   - Individual spiritual direction with a mentor
   - Ritual of beginning final stage
4. Celebration of the Sacrament
5. Postcelebration Ministries
   - Small communities
   - Continued involvement in youth ministry programs
   - Youth leadership training
   - Young adult and other parish ministries
   - Retreats

MARRIAGE
(Couples, Families, and Witnesses)

1. Evangelization
   - Visits with parish priest
   - Premarriage inventory
2. Catechesis
   - Rite of engagement
   - Topics to be covered: love as a decision and as a vow, marriage as friendship, marriage as covenant, marriage as a sign (sacrament), nurturing marriage
3. Proximate Preparation
   - Sessions with the celebrant to cover papers and liturgy
   - Sunday: blessing for preparation (banns)
4. Celebration of the Sacrament
5. Postcelebration Ministries
   - Small communities
   - Support programs on marriage and family life
   - Adult education
   - Retreats

7
Evangelizing Catechesis

This chapter is intended to be an overview of the catechesis the parish can offer to returning members. There is no such thing as the ideal process. The fabric and texture of parishes—based in part on socioeconomic makeup, education, ethnicity, race, devotionalism, and the like—are too diverse for any one process to fit all parishes. Aids and resources can be used for the reconciliation process, but that process must be customized for the people who are going through it and the community sponsoring it.

This chapter will help you design faith-formation sessions which are based on (1) the participants' own experiences—their hurts, needs, and questions; (2) the Scripture readings as laid out in the *Lectionary* or other passages that will draw out the participants' stories; and (3) the mysteries expressed in the Creed.

Remember, catechesis presumes preevangelization and evangelization. But there are no clean breaks between the steps. They often overlap. So, preevangelization, evangelization, and catechesis (particularly in our North American culture) are often going on all at the same time.

Michael Warren, in *Youth and the Future of the Church*, suggests that in catechesis, we as ministers seek to give witness to the presence of a transforming relationship in our lives.

That relationship is with Jesus who leads us to the Father, to the Spirit, to the community, and to justice as a way of life.

ADDRESSING THE PARTICIPANTS' EXPERIENCES

Any catechetical process that attempts to bypass the personal experiences of the participants will either fail or be reduced to a mental exercise (a consequence that may be worse than simple failure). The way to avoid that trap is to make absolutely certain that the participants have the opportunity to express their experiences—positive and negative—at every step of the way. Two kinds of experience are of particular importance for the reconciling believer: personal hurts or wounds and basic questions—usually questions that reveal needs.

Hurts and Wounds

Fritz Perls, a psychiatrist, was a leading force in the propagation of Gestalt therapy. The goal of Gestalt is the awareness of all that is going on within and around the self. Perls felt that the human personality is made up of five layers. Simply put, as each layer is stripped away, the subject of therapy gets closer and closer to healing and self-understanding. The first layer (cliché) involves very little investment of the self. The second layer (role-playing) consists of the many roles that a personality collects over the passage of time. The third layer (impasse) is a defense layer. Most people do not want anyone to penetrate this layer uninvited. The fourth layer (implosive/explosive) is an awareness of feelings and emotions that are either expressed (exploded) or repressed (imploded), or not dealt with. The fifth and final layer is the layer of genuine personality—stripped of defenses and artificialities. It is the goal of therapy to help a person get to these deeper levels, to understand them, and to live them. But understanding begins with the more superficial levels.

The catechist in the reconciling community needs to be aware that people come to the process with hurts, wounds, and scars. Part of the catechetical goal is to get to the layers of hurt and alienation that often lie hidden or repressed beneath an impasse layer. In the book *The Evangelizing Parish*, I discussed the doctoral research of John Savage, who has studied the phenomenon of alienation from the believing community in many denominations. Savage puts forth the notion that no matter what the symptoms or stories told by the alienated members, there are other more personal, more painful stories underneath. To borrow Perls's imagery, alienated members may talk about why they left the Church from the cliché, role-playing, or impasse layers. In fact, they are concealing more profound pain in the deeper layers of their personalities. These hurts often center in the psychological, in memory, in relationships, in vocation or occupation, or in specific areas that the person is unwilling to analyze.

Throughout the reconciling community process, sponsors and others need to help participants face these deeper areas of painful memory. But this must be done gently. Most sponsors and other ministers in the process will not have therapeutic skills. It is enough that they communicate that there is nothing to fear from these old hurts and wounds. Facing these feelings can be liberating and refreshing.

The obvious question is "How can untrained sponsors or other ministers help the returnees get in touch with these deeper levels?" John Savage suggests that the best (and safest) way to do this is through the sharing of stories. Storytelling helps people get in touch with different dimensions of their histories and their lives. The more stories that are shared, the more the real areas of hurt or brokenness will be revealed. Reconciliation is the healing of such hurt. And the beginning of healing is the naming of these hurts.

Early in the process, the stories people tell will be the stories at the cliché level—how the institutional Church has wounded them. A simple way of inviting people into a deeper level of the healing process is to have them write their responses to the following questions:

1. What prompted you to come to these sessions?

2. Did you have negative experiences with a parish, the Church in general, or a church-related person? Did these experiences hurt or anger you?

3. Do you have any expectations of the Church or your local parish that are not being met?

Father John Forliti of the diocese of Saint Paul and Minneapolis created a process of reconciliation for the inactive believer called Alienated Catholics Anonymous. He takes participants through a series of healing steps similar to those of Alcoholics Anonymous. The first step is to admit that one has a problem with the Church or parish. The second is to break the problem down and to identify specific hurts. The third step is to make a commitment to prayer for inner healing. Such healing prayer can even include a prayer for one's enemies—specifically for people who have been the source of hurt. Praying for one's enemies has proven to have a healing effect on participants.

Needs and Questions

One strategy I use in sacramental formation, RCIA work, or working with the reconciling community is to ask participants at the beginning of the journey to write down some of their questions about God, life, religion, or spirituality. Because they will write these questions or issues anonymously, the participants will not have to worry about appearing stupid or foolish in the group. The team then sifts through the questions and arranges them in some meaningful order for future discussion. Starting with participants' questions is a good way to do evangelization. It is, in effect, meeting people where they are at in their spiritual journey.

A similar technique can be used to bring the needs of the participants to the surface. By needs, I mean those felt or real social, spiritual, liturgical, or moral hungers and thirsts that can be met at the parish level.

But dealing with such needs and questions can raise the anxiety level of the ministering team, especially the ministers of the Word. How are volunteer ministers, with little theological background, to prepare for discussions on life's deepest mysteries or questions about Church or doctrine? Among the best resources for helping ministers deal with these matters are Richard McBrien's *Catholicism,* Bernard Marthaler's *The Creed,* and the German Catechetical Association's *Credo: A Catholic Catechism.*

PRAYING AND STUDYING THE SCRIPTURES

In some parishes, the reconciling community meets on a weekday before the Sunday Eucharist. In other parishes, the community gathers on Sunday, attends the Liturgy of the Word, is dismissed, and reconvenes in another place to discuss the Scriptures. Whether a group uses the Sunday *Lectionary* or some other passages suggested by the ministering team, similar strategies can be employed to pray and study the Scriptures.

In all of the following models, it would be most effective to stimulate the imaginations of the participants as they reflect on the Scriptures. Ignatius's method of imagining oneself as playing a role in the Scripture stories can be helpful. Remember: Evangelization needs to speak to the imagination.

An African Model

Some of the following steps are used in catechumenate work in the villages of Africa.

1. The session is begun with prayer, formal or informal.

2. The Scriptures are read slowly and deliberately. Those in attendance are invited to listen for words and phrases that strike them or stand out for them.

3. There is a pause for silence.

4. Each person shares with the group the word or phrase that has special meaning for him or her.

5. The Scriptures are read again.

6. The group is given about five minutes of silence to "sit with the text." Then, the participants write a response to these questions: "What do I hear in my heart? How do these Scriptures touch my life today?"

7. The large group is divided into smaller groups. In the small groups, participants share their answers, using the pronoun *I* ("I feel" or "I think"). The sharing, however, is not a discussion or a problem-solving session. It is a revelation, a sharing of inner experiences.

8. The Scriptures are read a third time.

9. The participants write answers to the following questions: "What does God want me to do or to be this week? How is God inviting me to change this week? What am I taking home this week?"

10. The participants share their answers in the small groups.

11. The session is closed with a prayer.

The Lumko Institute

The "Look-Listen-Love" method was discussed in chapter 5, but it is mentioned here in the context of Scripture study. It is during the Listen step that relevant Scripture passages are proclaimed, and time is given for silent reflection on God's Word. The participants then share what God is saying to them through human experience and Scripture. The goal of this procedure is to help participants live the Gospel and act on God's Word in the coming week.

Saint Augustine Church

Father Ray Kemp served for years at Saint Augustine Church in Washington, D.C. Father Kemp has become well known around the country for his pastoral wisdom and expertise in catechumenal processes. Basically, Father Kemp implements the African model discussed earlier, but he adds the following questions:

1. What did you hear? (What thoughts, phrases, and images stood out from Scripture?)

2. What does it mean? (Why did certain thoughts, phrases, and images strike you? Were there events in your life that were somewhat similar to the events in the Scripture readings? What questions do the Scriptures raise about life, faith, or Church?)

3. What will it cost you to live the message of today's Scripture? (What are you being called to? What are the obstacles to living the call?)

The results of the questions and reflection are shared in small groups, and then in the large group. The session closes with prayer.

FOCUSING ON THE CREED

Doctrinal language is a summary and symbolic way of capturing life-changing realities. The original meaning of the word *credo* is "I give my heart to." Both of these notions—the life-changing realities and the affective nature of what one professes to believe—are important to an understanding of the Creed. The Creed was never meant to become a cerebral, intellectual, "dry as dust," rote recitation of religious truths or information. Traditionally, the Creed is a heartfelt profession of truth and realities that have a profound effect on the mind, heart, and behavior of the believer. One of the signs of a converting or a reconciling Christian is the ability to recite meaningfully and with great conviction the Creed in the context of the eucharistic assembly.

The following Study Guide consists of model sessions that can help the reconciling community focus on the mysteries of the Creed. The sessions are designed according to the principles and methodology of adult learning theory and are offered here as an aid to communities who are designing their own reconciling process.

STUDY GUIDE
Remember, Return, and Rebirth

SESSION 1: We believe in the face of mystery.

First Journal Activity

Across the top of a sheet of paper, list in chronological order the years since you graduated from high school. If it is easier, do it in multiples of five (for example, 1965, 1970, 1975, 1980, 1985). Now, for each year you list, write a brief response to these four questions:

1. What was happening in the world?
2. What was going on in your personal life?
3. What was your image of God?
4. What was your relationship to the Church?

After you have completed your chart, share parts of it with your sponsor or small group.

Reflection

The following material can be read quietly in your small group or used as the basis for a talk by a catechist.

> Falling in love, a bout with illness, a tragedy that we hear about on the news, a natural disturbance that causes us both awe and fear—all are examples of mystery. Many

years ago, the word *mystery* might have been used as an automatic response to shut down conversation about things that could not be explained. But today, the use of the word *mystery* is different. We know now that mysteries are real; they are experiences in which we find ourselves over our heads, not in control, not knowing how things are going to turn out.

Mystery brings us to the very nub of existence. We either collapse in the face of mystery (collapse with mistrust, anxiety, fear, competition, or despair), or through the mystery, we discover a new energy, a new power for life. Rabbi Harold Kushner speaks of this in his books *When Bad Things Happen to Good People* and *When Everything You Always Wanted Isn't Enough*. When mystery takes on a painful facade, we need to remember that God is not the cause of the pain or tragedy associated with the mystery. Human life carries within itself a given amount of difficulty and pain. Rather than being the cause of difficulty and pain, God, according to the revelation of Jesus, is our source of courage, strength, and healing. The keys to the inner consolation that God brings are prayerfulness and faithfulness.

Because God is our help and hope in the pain of mystery and is present with us in the joyful moments of mystery, we can say that the human experiences that constitute mystery are actual meeting places with God —times when God speaks to us. Sometimes, God's message is one of comfort. At other times, the message is one of challenge. God's Word is not just found in Scripture; it is also found in the fabric of human experiences. We begin to hear God's Word when we begin to envision God as a loving parent, and when we begin to pray from the heart, personally, and in a posture of quiet and listening.

Second Journal Activity

Share your answers to the following questions with your sponsor or small group.

1. What are some of your emotional reactions to the above reflection?
2. Look back at the chart in the First Journal Activity. Were there any times when God was especially present and active in your life? What were they?
3. How has your concept of God changed over the years?

Large-Group Sharing

Gather together in one large group, and discuss the main points that were shared at the end of the Second Journal Activity.

Scripture

Have someone from the group proclaim Exodus 3:1–12. After the Scripture reading, pause for a moment of silence.

Prayer

Conclude the session by saying the following prayer together:

> Lord, through the burning bush, you called Moses to live life in a new way. You called him to a new direction. Through the burning bushes, the mysteries of our lives, call us and help us become our best selves. Reassure us with your words to Moses: "I will be with you." Amen.

SESSION 2: We believe in God the Father (Parent), creator of heaven and earth.

First Journal Activity
Answer the following, and then share your thoughts and feelings with your sponsor or small group.
1. List as many characteristics as you can of an ideal, effective parent.
2. Are there some characteristics of parenting that belong exclusively to a father? If so, what are they?
3. Are there some characteristics of parenting that belong exclusively to a mother? If so, what are they?
4. List any of the characteristics that you feel apply to the personal force that is traditionally called God the Father.

Reflection
The following material can be read quietly in your small group, or it can be used as the basis for a talk by a catechist.

> The doctrine of the Trinity is a human attempt to describe how Christians have experienced God over the centuries. There have been three dominant experiences in our tradition: God as parent of all and creator of life; Jesus, God's Son, who has redeemed and is redeeming a lost world by his teaching, death, and resurrection; and the Holy Spirit, the force, power, and energy of God's presence and love present among us today.
>
> Sometimes it takes an experience like the ones described in the reflection on mystery to lead us to really believe (give our hearts) to a God of love. We have all grown up in families—some of them happy, others not. If family memories have been painful, belief in an all-loving parent can entail a difficult leap of the imagination. But sometimes life experiences bring us down to the very nub of things: Is life worth living? Do I want to go on? What is the meaning of life?
>
> One of the core teachings of Jesus is that throughout life we are in the presence and love of an abiding Someone, whom Jesus called *Abba*, a loving term for "Father." Jesus wanted people of all times to know that life is indeed

worth living and that it is meaningful because of God the loving Parent, who cares for us and forgives us. Jesus himself was so convinced of this that he accepted the suffering of the cross, convinced that the power of God's love could transform pain and disaster into new life. Jesus teaches us that we ought to relax more and to live in a spirit of trust, surrender, and cooperation with God. Even while dying on the cross, Jesus expressed his profound trust by praying, "Father, into your hands I commend my spirit" *(Luke 23:46)*. The same courage for life that Jesus had can at least in part be ours, if we learn to pray with trust and surrender as he did.

For years, many of us have heard too much about a punishing, authoritarian God. Though Jesus occasionally speaks of God's wrath or anger, he more often speaks of God as a loving parent whom we ought to love and trust. For years, too, we heard a rather negative interpretation of the Genesis creation accounts. The "fall" of Adam and Eve was certainly stressed more vigorously than the positive view of God who began the process of creation, made all of life good, and continues to sustain and nurture the universe.

We need to spend moments each day in wonder at God's good creation. We also need to realize that the process of creation, begun by God, is continuing now through each of us. Either we can be irresponsible with the gifts of creation, destroying or distorting them through negligence, sin, or pollution, or we can realize we are cocreators with God. As cocreators we need to reverence and use well the gifts of the earth. Let us give our hearts to the God that Jesus revealed —the loving Parent, the Creator. Let us cease participating in the practice of creating our own images of God and engaging in contemporary idol worship.

Second Journal Activity

Share your answers to the following questions with your sponsor or small group.

1. How did Jesus show through his words and actions that he viewed God as the loving Parent and Creator?
2. Why do you think Jesus' positive God image angered the religious leaders of the age?
3. How do your family experiences—past and current—influence the way you imagine God?

Large-Group Sharing

Gather together in one large group and discuss the main points that were shared at the end of the Second Journal Activity. Feel free to add any thoughts you may have had during the Reflection.

Scripture

Have someone from the group proclaim Genesis 1:1–31 and Matthew 6:25–34. After the readings, pause for a moment of silence.

Prayer

Conclude the session by saying the following prayer from the Easter Vigil liturgy together:

> Almighty and eternal God, you created all things in wonderful beauty and order. Help us now to perceive how still more wonderful is the new creation by which, in the fullness of time, you redeemed your people through the sacrifice of our passover, Jesus Christ, who lives and reigns for ever and ever. Amen.

SESSION 3: We believe in Jesus, God's Son, our Lord, who was crucified, died, and was buried.

First Journal Activity

Answer the following, and then share your thoughts and feelings with your sponsor or small group.

1. Jesus perceived himself as God's Son. How do you think that made him feel?
2. What does "Jesus is Lord!" mean to you?
3. Describe the type of person you feel Jesus was—physically, emotionally, interpersonally.

Reflection

The following material can be read quietly in your small group, or it can be used as the basis for a talk by a catechist.

> To call someone *Lord* is to give a tremendous amount of authority to that person. *Lord* speaks of someone who has become a standard, or model—a source of truth, direction, and guidance. When we call Jesus *Lord,* we are saying that about him. His teaching, wisdom, and person have become authoritative and normative for us. Someone once described Jesus as the North Star, a marker by which one finds direction. Jesus' value as a marker for us comes from his own understanding of himself as God's Son. Jesus' experience of the Father was one of intimacy, oneness, communion. The indwelling Spirit of God—Abba—"made Jesus tick," motivated him. As the Father loves all people, Jesus taught, so we must love and relate to one another.
>
> The term Jesus used most frequently to hand on the vision, or outlook on life, that he felt the Father wishes us to live was *kingdom,* or *reign of God.* The reign of God was and is both a vision of reality and a way of living. In other words, it is not enough just to understand or to talk about the values of Jesus. True spiritual conversion also means changing one's behavior.
>
> Kingdom living begins with a change of mind and heart that recognizes the Father as the true authority in life, the life giver, the creator. Jesus' authority derives from his being the way to the Father, and the truth about living,

dying, relating, and God. Jesus is the revelation of the way the Father is and the way we ought to be. Perhaps the chief characteristics of kingdom living are love, compassion, equality, and justice. The kingdom of God is no less than the gradual transformation of the world toward a new creation of brotherly and sisterly love.

It was because of his kingdom preaching and teaching that Jesus suffered and died. The close, available God that Jesus taught was a threat to the religious leaders of the time, who had turned religion into a heavily legalistic experience. Jesus must have also threatened the Roman political leaders. Jesus' movement was becoming increasingly grass roots, attracting multitudes. The charismatic leadership of Jesus was threatening the control that both political and religious leaders held over people. Jesus had to go!

The religious leaders conspired to have Jesus legally convicted of insurrection. The penalty: crucifixion. Crucifixion was a Roman form of torture and execution. Surprisingly, scientists have revealed in recent years that death from crucifixion resulted not so much from blood loss as from asphyxiation—crucified people just could not get air. To hasten death, soldiers would break the legs of people on a cross so that they could not push themselves up to gasp air. They did not have to do that for Jesus, since he died relatively quickly. His quick death would seem to indicate that he was rather badly bruised and hurt prior to his crucifixion. He was hastily buried in a grave donated by Joseph of Arimathea.

Jesus had prophetically stated several times that death would not be the end of him, that the Father's power could turn even failure, defeat, and death into something new. Those leaving his grave that Friday afternoon must have wondered what he meant.

Second Journal Activity

Read the following, and then share your answers with your sponsor or small group.

1. Allan Bloom, in *The Closing of the American Mind*, wrote that there is a lot of religious affiliation or church membership in America, but that religion does not seem to influence people's lives a great deal. Comment on what he might have meant.
2. Like Jesus, each of us lives, dies, and rises in small ways daily. Explain what this means to you.
3. A feast called the Triumph of the Cross is celebrated on September 14. How can Jesus, or anyone, triumph through a cross?

Large-Group Sharing

Gather together in one large group, and discuss the main points shared in the Second Journal Activity. Try to summarize in your own words the main ideas in the Reflection.

Scripture

Have someone from the group proclaim Luke 23:44–49. After the reading, pause for a moment of silence.

Prayer

Conclude the session by saying the following prayer from the Good Friday liturgy together:

> Almighty and eternal God, you have restored us to life by the triumphant death and resurrection of Christ. Continue this healing work with us. May we who participate in this mystery never cease to serve you. We ask this in the name of Jesus the Lord. Amen.

SESSION 4: We believe in the Holy Spirit, the Lord, the giver of life, who proceeds from the Father and the Son.

First Journal Activity

Answer the following questions, and then share your thoughts and feelings with your sponsor or small group.

1. With the exception of Catholic charismatic groups, many Catholics and other Christians seem more comfortable with God the Father and with Jesus than with the Holy Spirit. Why do you feel or think that is the case?
2. If you had to describe the experience of the Holy Spirit to a total unbeliever, what would you say?
3. In what way do the gifts of the Holy Spirit—wisdom, understanding, judgment, courage, knowledge, reverence, wonder and awe—influence your life?

Reflection

The following material can be read quietly in your small group, or it can be used as the basis for a talk by a catechist.

> Have you noticed the "look of love" that sometimes exists between an old couple? There seems to be almost an energy force—a passion, an electricity, a magnetism—in the way the old man and old woman look at each other. The force, of course, is the force of love. A few years ago, when the movie *Star Wars* was popular, talk about "the force" was rather prevalent. "The force" was seen as a kind of "good energy" that worked on the side of the "good guys."
>
> The love between a committed older couple and the force of good portrayed in the movies can be used to describe the Holy Spirit. The Holy Spirit is the love and presence of the Father and Jesus extending to us in our own day. The Holy Spirit is how we experience and relate to God each day. The way we most profoundly experience the Holy Spirit is by opening our minds and hearts in personal, heartfelt prayer. Sometimes life situations simply demand that we very deliberately pray "Come, Holy Spirit." When people do experience the Spirit, they report

different kinds of things happening to them: a new courage for life, new direction, wisdom where there was only confusion, challenge where there was complacency, forgiveness and reconciliation where there was alienation, and on and on.

In addition to conscious attempts to invoke and invite the Holy Spirit into our hearts, sometimes we have a different experience with the Spirit. Sometimes people report having a feeling of being *grasped* by something more than themselves. Different trigger experiences can make this happen: a beautiful sunset, a song, a loving relationship, a painful crisis. Spiritual growth, then, is not always our doing. Sometimes God, working through human experiences, grasps and changes us. And this always happens in and through the Holy Spirit.

It would be good if Christians became more familiar with the Holy Spirit. The experience of the Holy Spirit is at the heart of what the Church is about. The Church was not really born until the first Pentecost. On that day, the Apostles were hiding in fear in an upper room. When they were "grasped" by the Spirit, Peter stood up to evangelize, to tell other people how the Lord had changed his life. His testimony led about three thousand people to convert and to be baptized. They formed themselves into small communities, sharing prayer, Scripture, and the Lord's Supper (see Acts 2).

Maybe the Christian churches would benefit from a true back-to-basics movement—a movement that emphasizes the Holy Spirit, conversion joined to the sacraments, gentle and honest evangelizing, and genuine community.

Second Journal Activity

Share your answers to the following questions with your sponsor or small group.

1. Have you or someone you know ever had a Pentecost-type experience? Describe what it was like.
2. Are there any circumstances that prompt you to pray to the Holy Spirit very deliberately and consciously? What are they?
3. In your own words, describe the Holy Spirit.

Large-Group Sharing

Get together in one large group, and spend some time summarizing the main ideas of the Second Journal Activity, the Reflection, and any other input.

Scripture

Have someone from the group proclaim Acts 2:1–15, 22–23, 37–42. After the reading, pause for a moment of silence.

Prayer

Conclude the session by saying the following prayer:

> God our Father, let the Spirit be sent on your Church to begin the teaching of the Gospel. Continue to work in the world through the hearts of all who believe. We ask this through our Lord Jesus Christ, your Son, who lives and reigns with you and the Holy Spirit, one God for ever and ever. Amen.

SESSION 5: We believe in Jesus, born of Mary.

First Journal Activity

Answer the following questions, and then share your thoughts and feelings with your sponsor or small group.

1. The Catholic Church has given more emphasis to Mary than some of the other Christian groups. Right now, what are your thoughts and feelings about devotion to Mary?
2. What are some Marian activities that you recall doing when you were a child?
3. Is the contemporary Church giving adequate attention to Mary? What changes would you recommend, if any?

Reflection

The following material can be read quietly in your small group, or it can be used as the basis for a talk by a catechist.

> Experts now say that Mary was probably in her early teens when she gave birth to Jesus. It was not unusual for women of such tender years to be betrothed to be married. In Mary's day, families were influential in arranging marriages; thus Mary was betrothed to Joseph. The discussion abounds as to how Mary became pregnant with Jesus. The Catholic tradition holds to the virgin birth of Jesus and to the belief that Jesus was conceived by the Holy Spirit. Virginal conception through the power of the Holy Spirit speaks loudly and clearly that the birth of Mary's child was a special, history-changing event.
>
> People who claim that devotion to Mary is a late distortion in the evolution of Christianity simply do not know history. Devotion to Mary dates back to the early Christian centuries. What is true is that perhaps in the Middle Ages, and later still among people of simple faith, Mary sometimes received more attention than Jesus did. This certainly was not a deliberate attempt at idolatry. Rather, it was the result of poor, often illiterate, peasant people trying to have some kind of spiritual life. But without the ability to read the Scriptures, psalms, and prayer books, as the educated clergy did, they resorted to simple forms of devotion, often to the Mother of Jesus.

There was also a whole spirituality of unworthiness tied in with some expressions of Marian devotion. People felt unworthy to go to God directly, to Jesus directly. So, they went indirectly to the divine through Mary or, if not Mary, one of the saints. Poorly trained clergy and poorly informed laity perpetuated the distortions from generation to generation. It is important to keep in mind, however, that even in these wrong emphases, there was much goodwill, devotion, and faith.

What are we to make of Mary today, then? Mary is a model disciple, a person deliberately and consciously following Jesus, even to the foot of the cross. She is the God bearer; she physically carried Jesus before birth, and nurtured and raised him. Mary reminds us to assume the identities of disciple and God bearer. She mirrors profound faith to the contemporary world. Much of what came into Mary's life she did not understand at the time. But she accepted many life situations cooperatively, believing God was with her. She always struggled to do what she perceived as God's will. Mary is a healthy example of cooperating with others and God.

As people may still speak to the spirit of a deceased loved one, so also it is appropriate to commune and communicate with the spirit of Mary and all the saints, asking them to speak to God with us and for us. This is not idol worship but an example of what is meant by the communion of saints. We, here on earth, are in communion with Mary, the saints, and our loved ones who have died. Among those special people who have been glorified with God in eternal life, Mary holds the preeminent place.

Second Journal Activity

Answer the following questions, and then share your thoughts and feelings with your sponsor or small group.

1. What are two or three images of Mary that have most affected your own journey of faith?
2. If you could sit down and talk with Mary, what are two questions you would ask?

Large-Group Sharing

Get together in one large group, and try to summarize the main ideas from the Second Journal Activity, the Reflection, and any other input.

Scripture

Have someone from the group proclaim Luke 1:46–56. After the reading, pause for a moment of silence.

Prayer

Conclude the session by joining hands and saying the following prayer.

> Hail, Mary, full of grace, the Lord is with thee. Blessed art thou among women, and blessed is the fruit of thy womb, Jesus. Holy Mary, Mother of God, pray for us sinners, now, and at the hour of our death. Amen.

SESSION 6: We believe in one, holy, catholic, and apostolic Church.

First Journal Activity
Answer the following, and then share your thoughts and feelings with your sponsor or small group.
1. Record some happy memories that you have of the Church. (Recall school, CCD, parish involvement, or "church people" who positively influenced you.)
2. Record some hurting memories (negative events or people) that you have of the Church.

Reflection
The following material can be read quietly in your small group, or it can be used as the basis for a talk by a catechist.

> Much thinking and writing have taken place over the years regarding *ecclesiology,* a term that might be foreign to you. Ecclesiology refers to one's outlook or vision of Church. In other words, what is the Church supposed to be? One theologian, Avery Dulles, has lined up a number of ways to describe the Church. In his book entitled *Models of the Church,* he says the Church is a *living sacrament* (or sign) of God's presence in the world, a *herald* (or teacher) of the truth, a *prophet* challenging the world, an experience of *communion* with God, and a worldwide *institution.*
>
> In a later book, *A Church to Believe In,* Dulles adds that there is an even more primitive model of Church that we need to return to. That model is the one that the first disciples and Apostles experienced: *a community of disciples* following and being mentored or taught by Jesus and the Holy Spirit.
>
> Discipleship, or a community of disciples, is a notion many people who were raised in the Catholic Church or in mainline Protestant churches are rather unfamiliar with. Yet, says Dulles, it is the most primitive form of Church. The disciples, as portrayed in the four Gospels, were adults following Jesus on a journey—the pursuit of truth. Many people listened to Jesus, but the disciples felt a personal

call to follow Jesus in intense learning. The goal of their learning was not information or content. Rather, they were trying to learn of the values of Jesus, what he meant when he spoke of life in the kingdom of God. The disciples, in turn, began to multiply the effect Jesus was having on the world by continuing his work, both while he was still on earth and after his ascension into glory.

If we as the contemporary Church are to become a community of disciples, we must take on a life-style similar to that of the original discipling community. A personal relationship with Jesus—one in which we appropriate his values, continue his mission in our own families and homes, and imitate his acts of service—must become our felt responsibility.

Such a shift, from a heavily institutional model of Church to a more disciple-oriented Church, is bringing a great deal of change to the Catholic Church. More and more people are becoming involved in ministries and leadership in their parishes. More Catholics are actively working on a deep, heartfelt prayer and spiritual life. They are beginning to see that the issues of social justice are intimately tied to being a spiritual person, that there is indeed a performance, or behavioral, component to faith. Many Catholics are seeking out small prayer and faith-sharing groups to give them support in living their faith in a world that is becoming increasingly hostile to the Christian vision. Unfortunately, with the Church becoming so alive in the Spirit, there is also a decline in the number of men and women seeking the priesthood and religious life.

The Church has gone through a number of shifts, twists, and turns in its two-thousand-year evolution. No doubt that evolution will continue. But we have the infallible assurance of Jesus that the Spirit will always be with us, guiding us toward truth, wisdom, and justice.

Second Journal Activity

Answer the following questions, and then share your thoughts and feelings with your sponsor or small group.

1. What are some of the positive changes that have taken place in the Catholic Church in the past twenty-five years?
2. In recent years, the American bishops have become increasingly involved in sociopolitical issues such as the economy, nuclear weapons, and women's rights. What are your feelings about these developments?

Large-Group Sharing

Get together in one large group, and try to summarize the main points from the Second Journal Activity, the Reflection, and any other input.

Scripture

Have someone from the group proclaim Ephesians 2:19–22. After the reading, pause for a moment of silence.

Prayer

Conclude the session by saying the following prayer from the feast of the Chair of Peter.

> All-powerful Father, you have built your Church on the rock of Saint Peter's confession of faith. May nothing divide or weaken our unity in faith and love. Grant this through our Lord Jesus Christ, your Son, who lives and reigns with you and the Holy Spirit, one God for ever and ever. Amen.

SESSION 7: We believe in Baptism and the other sacraments.

First Journal Activity

Answer the following, and then share your thoughts and feelings with your sponsor or small group.

1. Record some of your thoughts and feelings about a past sacramental celebration, for example, the baptism of a child, your own First Communion or reconciliation, confirmation, your marriage, or a possible anointing experience.
2. The Church continues to place great emphasis on regular attendance at and celebration of the Mass. In your own view, what is the importance of the Eucharist?

Reflection

The following material can be read quietly in your small group, or it can be used as the basis for a talk by a catechist.

> If you studied the Baltimore Catechism some years ago, you probably remember the term *sacraments* being described as "outward signs instituted by Christ to give grace." Many of us grew up with an understanding of sacraments as *signs* of something *more*, something *mysterious*, a sign of the *divine*, a sign of God's influence active in the human story. History reveals, however, that the word *sacrament* has a more ancient connotation than that of *sign*.
>
> The original meaning of the word *sacramentum* was "vow." The early Church borrowed the word *sacramentum* from the Roman military, for whom it meant "a pledge or vow to live or die for the Roman emperor." The early Christian community applied the word to its ancient rites of initiation, which included Baptism, Eucharist, and what is now known as Confirmation as three moments in one event—the initiation and rebirth of new Christians. This rather lengthy ceremony, which, in the third century, came to be celebrated on Holy Saturday night and early Easter morning, included immersion in water (Baptism), anointing with chrism (now known as Confirmation), and reception of First Communion (Eucharist). From these

early rituals of the Church, the seven sacred rituals, now called sacraments, have evolved.

Many Catholics have a poor understanding of that last statement. Indeed, the sacraments have changed shape and form over the centuries. Some of the shifts and changes are noted below.

Baptism. In the early Church, Baptism was most often celebrated by adults as a sign of conversion. Gradually the focus shifted, beginning especially in the fourth and fifth centuries, to the baptism of children. The doctrine of original sin, which precluded unbaptized infants who died from entering heaven, seems to have propagated the emphasis on children. Since the 1970s, the Catholic Church has had a kind of two-tract approach: a continuation of the baptism of infants, while also encouraging the conversion of adults joined to Baptism.

Confirmation. Gradually, part of the initiation ceremony—the bishop's laying on of hands and his anointing of candidates with chrism (chrismation)—became separate from the baptism ritual. More and more centers of Christianity spoke of this anointing ceremony as a separate ritual, with a separate theology (a new coming of the Holy Spirit). By the eleventh century, it was popularly accepted as a separate event. It was officially declared a sacrament at the Council of Lyons in 1274. While many theologies of Confirmation abound, it is best understood as the completion of Baptism or initiation.

Eucharist. The first version of the Mass was a brief fellowship meal, celebrated in homes. The first Christians celebrated both Eucharist and Jewish synagogue services. Over a period of time, the early Christians moved from the Saturday celebration to Sunday to mark the resurrection. The celebration began with something like the Liturgy of the Word (prayer and Scripture). Later in the day, the meal was shared. Eventually, the two components—Word and meal—were joined in one ceremony. Having been moved out of homes and into basilicas and churches, the meal dimension became largely symbolic in nature. During the Middle Ages, the Eucharist was largely understood as a "holy thing" that only priests could touch and that most people did not deserve to receive frequently. The Council of Trent, in the sixteenth century, structured the Mass as it was to remain until the reforms of Vatican II. Around the turn of the twentieth century, Pope Pius X encouraged small children (age seven) to receive the Eucharist. Up to this point, the common age for first reception was fourteen.

Reconciliation. The early Christians adapted the Jewish penitential practice of fasting, public penance, almsgiving, and so on. When a number who had defected from the Church to avoid persecution wanted to rejoin, church leaders devised a process of return which was based on the process of initiation. This process involved a confession of sin, years of penance, and a celebration of acceptance back into the community on Holy Thursday. This process of reconciliation is the early version of our sacrament of Penance, which consists of Scripture reading, confession, prayers of sorrow, acceptance of penance, and changed living after the ritual. Since 1976 there have been three styles of celebrating Reconciliation: one-on-one with a priest, one-on-one with a priest in the context of a prayer service, and general absolution (when circumstances make it necessary). The private confession format began in the sixth century, largely through the influence of Irish monks.

Anointing of the Sick. For years this sacrament was understood as Extreme Unction: anointing the body and senses before death. Since Vatican II, the original meaning of the ritual, as spoken of in chapter 5 of the Letter of James, has been retrieved—calling on God for healing and mercy for the suffering and sick.

Matrimony. The first Christians married in civil ceremonies. They became "married in the Lord" either through their own intentionality or by inviting the bishop or a priest to attend the ceremony. By the fifth century, there was a ritual for marriage in the Church. By the eleventh century, marriage was popularly regarded as a sacrament.

Holy Orders. In the early Church, there was a variety of ministries: priest, prophet, teacher, deacon, deaconess, widow, bishop, and so on. Gradually, an ordained ministry evolved that included the pope, bishops, priests, and deacons. (In recent years, the order of deacon has been restored as a permanent one.)

The seven sacred rituals called sacraments were defined at the second Council of Lyons (1274), the Council of Florence (1439), and the Council of Trent (1547). Though the Catholic Church recognizes these sacred seven, any person or experience can be sacramental in the sense that the person or experience communicates or reveals God's presence.

Second Journal Activity

Answer the following questions, and then share your thoughts and feelings with your sponsor or small group.

1. What new thoughts about sacraments have emerged for you from the foregoing history?
2. Besides the sacred seven, has anyone or anything ever functioned sacramentally for you, that is, communicated a sense of God's presence?

Large-Group Sharing

Get together in one large group, and try to summarize the main points from the Second Journal Activity, the Reflection, and any other input.

Scripture

Have someone from the group proclaim Romans 6:3–4, 8–9. After the reading, pause for a moment of silence.

Prayer

Conclude the session by saying the following prayer from the feast of Corpus Christi:

> Lord, may the bread and cup we offer bring your Church the unity and peace they signify. We ask this in the name of Jesus, the Lord. Amen.

SESSION 8: We believe in the forgiveness of sins.

First Journal Activity
Answer the following questions, and then share your thoughts and feelings with your sponsor or small group.

1. Recall your feelings from the past about sin, guilt, and going to confession. What are some of them? Are they positive or negative feelings?
2. Recent research shows the number of people using the sacrament of Reconciliation has significantly declined. Why do you think this is happening?

Reflection
The following material can be read quietly in your small group, or it can be used as the basis for a talk by a catechist.

> Chapters 3–11 of Genesis have been called by Scripture scholars the *harmartiology,* a technical term for a study of sin. The great stories of Adam and Eve, Cain and Abel, Noah and the Great Flood, and the Tower of Babel—all attempt to describe the meaning of sin. All of the stories make the same point: Sin is not just an isolated action. Sin is also an attitude. The attitude disposes people to actions that are contrary to God's Law—actions that are destructive of self, of others, of life itself. As a result, *sin* (attitude) leads to *sins* (behavioral). The result of sin, according to the Genesis stories, is alienation—alienation from one's best self, from others, or from God. The attitudes of sin, at root, are idolatrous, hostile, and irresponsible. Sin is *idolatry*—giving someone or something the center position in life that only God deserves. Sin is *hostility;* most often it expresses itself in acts of power and aggression. Sin is *irresponsibility.* Life is a gift, for which each person is responsible. Sin is irresponsibility for the gift of life.
>
> The prophets added to these early insights into sin, announcing that sin can become systemic, influencing whole organizations and nations. The prophets called not just individuals but the whole nation to corporate conversion. Jesus rearticulated the Old Testament notion of the subtle, attitudinal nature of sin. Jesus taught that it was

not externals but the interior, the heart of a person, that becomes corrupted by evil.

The Catholic tradition has built on the scriptural roots of sin, dividing sin into mortal and venial. Contemporary thought says that mortal sin is *deadly*, actually severing one's bond with the Lord. Venial sin would be anything less than that. Sin flows from *conscience*, or the moral judgment of a person. Conscience operates best proactively, that is, anticipating a decision or an action. One needs to engage in conscience formation before engaging in questionable attitudes or actions. More often, however, people use conscience retroactively, that is, they look back on an attitude or action in the past to discern its morality or immorality.

In conscience formation or discernment, there are a number of guides or helpers in the process: for example, the Ten Commandments, Jesus' great commandments of love, the Beatitudes, the teaching authority of the Church, trusted friends, and spiritual direction.

Part of conversion always includes repentance from sin. Repentance ought to be rooted in *contrition*, which is sorrow for sin that arises not out of guilt or fear but out of love. Contrition is sorrow for sin that flows from violating love, the relationship between a person and God, and the unconditional love God has for each individual.

One of the core revelations of Jesus is that God loves each person unconditionally and that one's sins are forgiven when he or she turns to God in repentance and contrition. The term *Good News* is often heard. One dimension of the Good News that the scribes and Pharisees had difficulty understanding was Jesus' conviction that God constantly offers people new beginnings.

Second Journal Activity

Answer the following questions, and then share your thoughts and feelings with your sponsor or small group.

1. Human beings are made in the image of God; they ought to be as God is. This includes having a loving, forgiving attitude toward others. Why are the words *I love you*, *I'm sorry*, and *I forgive you* so difficult for people to say to one another?
2. Are there relationships in your own life that are in need of repair or reconciliation? Name one, and describe something you can do to begin to heal it.

Large-Group Sharing

Get together in one large group, and try to summarize the main points from the Second Journal Activity, the Reflection, and any other input.

Scripture

Have someone from the group proclaim Luke 15:1–7. After the reading, pause for a moment of silence.

Prayer

Conclude the session by saying the following prayer.

> I confess to almighty God and to you, my brothers and sisters, that I have sinned through my own fault, in what I have done and in what I have failed to do. I ask blessed Mary, ever virgin, and you, my brothers and sisters, to pray for me to the Lord our God. Amen.

SESSION 9: We believe in the resurrection of the dead.

First Journal Activity
Answer the following questions, and then share your thoughts and feelings with your sponsor or small group.
1. Name the people closest to you whom you have lost through death. Which losses brought the greatest grief?
2. Novels, philosophy, movies—all have tried to depict what the afterlife is like. How do you envision it?

Reflection
The following material can be read quietly in your small group, or it can be used as the basis for a talk by a catechist.

> In his classic study *The Denial of Death*, Ernest Becker speaks of death as the one basic fear that every human being carries within. Much human activity, he says, is an attempt to escape the reality of death. People keep on moving in an attempt to avoid reflection on the reality— the inevitable reality of *stopping*. One of life's deepest paradoxes is that people are free to be totally alive only when they have faced death square in the face, accepting fully the "ultimate limit" that they will one day cease to have a corporeal existence.
>
> The modern era ushered in the existentialist movement, which maintains that the only reality is the here and now. According to this view, hope for an afterlife, or eternal life, as Christians describe it, is at best a dubious hope or an irrelevant issue, not subject for empirical scrutiny.
>
> However, as Jesus' short life progressed, it appears that his inevitable death was crucial for, and would be the centerpiece of, his mission. Jesus, in his early thirties, had to face and integrate the fact that he would die. Luke, the physician-evangelist, reports several times that Jesus moved "resolutely" toward Jerusalem. As a student of humanity, Luke presents Jesus as knowing the fatal conflict that awaited him in the mother city of Judaism, yet not flinching from it. Luke's picture of the last hours of Jesus' life shows Jesus experiencing a range of emotions. But the primary emotions are courage and surrender. With his

last breath, Jesus prayed Psalm 31, "Into your hands I commend my spirit."

The Judeo-Christian tradition is based on a paschal vision of life. The word *paschal* means "passage." The Sinai Covenant taught the Jews (and the first Christians) that passage is the very nature of things. All human life flows in a passage from life through death to new life.

The Christian passover—life through death to new life (resurrection)—means that life is forever. This passage theology expresses itself in at least three ways. First, the passage is expressed in the kind of growth and transformation that arise from personal crises (little deaths). Life does not always go according to plan. Gail Sheehy, in the book *Passages*, calls such times and experiences "life accidents." While some people give in to despair in the face of life accidents, Christians embrace them as Jesus would. They trust that the power of God joined to personal faith and cooperation can turn such crises into opportunities for growth and transformation. Such opportunities are little tastes of the eternal life that follows the final, physical death.

Second, the passage nature of life is also expressed in the growth and transformation that occur as the result of discipline or self-denial. All people have the experience of catching a glimpse of themselves in a mirror and disliking what they see. Saint Paul speaks of the experience of "putting to death" that within us which is not of the Lord *(Colossians 3:5)*. Growth or transformation sometimes involves choosing discipline (saying no to something). Curbing one's desires and behavior gives a person the chance to experience something new or better in relationships, in work, or in personal life. But this discipline, or death to self, is not just human effort. It is carried out in cooperation with God's healing and transforming love as the essential ingredients for a new and enriched life.

A third expression of the passage nature of Christian life is expressed in the leap of faith brought about by a brush with death. Because faith has helped us pass through life's accidents, and personally chosen areas of growth, we are better able to turn to faith when we either lose a loved one to death or we face death ourselves. Because we have tasted new life in small ways through human experiences, we make the leap of faith when physical death looks us in the eye. Just as death has given way to new life in other experiences, so also death gives way to eternal life in the face of death with a capital *D*.

Second Journal Activity

Answer the following questions, and then share your thoughts and feelings with your sponsor or small group.

1. What are some examples of a discipline (death to self) you have taken upon yourself in order to grow or become a better Christian?
2. Why is spiritual surrender so hard for most people? Why is surrender such a big part of resurrection?

Large-Group Sharing

Get together in one large group, and try to summarize the main points from the Second Journal Activity, the Reflection, and any other input.

Scripture

Have someone from the group proclaim 1 Corinthians 15:35–38, 42–44, 50–53. After the reading, pause for a moment of silence.

Prayer

Conclude with the following prayer.

> Let us call aloud the names of deceased people whom we would like to commend to the Lord. (Pause to allow time for this calling out.) Eternal rest give to them, O Lord, and let perpetual light shine upon them. May their souls, and all the souls of the faithful departed, rest in peace. Amen.

SESSION 10: We believe in the life of the world to come.

First Journal Activity
Answer the following questions, and then share your thoughts and feelings with your sponsor or small group.

1. What are some cultural trends (in society, politics, economics, Church, or the media) that affect you right now? What do these trends say about the future?
2. What does the Second Coming of Christ mean to you? How does this teaching affect your daily life?

Reflection
The following material can be read quietly in your small group, or it can be used as the basis for a talk by a catechist.

> The "life of the world to come" has more than one connotation. In one sense, it refers to the afterlife, or eternal life (session 9). In this session, other meanings are explored. The early Christian community was convinced that Christ would come again. In his early writing, Saint Paul expressed feelings that this second coming was just around the corner. When Jesus did not appear in a timely fashion, Paul changed his approach in later writings. Even so, from the first centuries of Christianity till today, there is an expectation that Christ will come again.
>
> Some thought has connected the Second Coming of Christ with the end of the world—the end of time. Opinion is divided as to the nature of that event. Some feel and fear that the Second Coming of Christ will be connected with the physical destruction of the world, precipitated by the destructive forces of the human family. Many see the worldwide proliferation of nuclear weapons as a sign that the end is near. Others have a more positive view of the Second Coming. For example, the paleontologist and theologian Pierre Teilhard de Chardin saw the possibility that the world is evolving gradually toward the kind of world that Jesus envisioned. Teilhard de Chardin felt that the end of time—the Second Coming—would be the human family reaching its potential and fulfilling the plan God had from the dawn of creation. In such a

view, earth and heaven would unite. The cosmic Christ would return to reign over a transformed universe.

Actually, both of these scenarios have merit, and therein lie both frightening and exciting realities. God has set us over creation as we know it. Because of our free will, we can be faithful stewards of creation, or we can be cancers that destroy creation. Human decisions and activities will largely determine whether the Second Coming of Christ will mean annihilation or glorification. Therefore, it is very important for each Christian to assume responsibility not only for his or her own life but also for the course of history—the quality of life, social justice, the equality of all people, and reverence for all life. The Church is a servant to the world. The mission of the Church is to nudge creation toward the fulfillment of God's purpose.

Second Journal Activity

Answer the following questions, and then share your thoughts and feelings with your sponsor or small group.

1. How do you react to the two views of the world to come? Which direction do you feel the world is taking? Explain what you mean.
2. What specific things can churches do to influence the future—to create a world that is on the way to fulfilling God's plan?

Large-Group Sharing

Get together in one large group, and try to summarize the main points from the Second Journal Activity, the Reflection, and any other input.

Scripture

Have someone from the group proclaim Matthew 25:31–46. After the reading, pause for a moment of silence.

Prayer

Conclude the session by praying the following prayer from the feast of Christ the King.

> Father, all powerful and ever-living God, we do well always and everywhere to give you thanks. You anointed Jesus Christ, your only Son, with the oil of gladness, as the eternal priest and universal king. As priest, he offered his life on the altar of the cross and redeemed the human race by this one perfect sacrifice of peace. As king, he claims dominion over all creation, that he may present to you, his almighty Father, an eternal and universal kingdom—a kingdom of truth and life, a kingdom of holiness and grace, a kingdom of justice, love, and peace.

EPILOGUE
Reflections and Critique from Experience

While people may have the spontaneous urge to return to God, to the Church, and to the Eucharist, I am convinced that most of them need some sort of process for reintegration into the community. The actual Reconciling Community experience may, in fact, touch very few. That is why I have included material on improving sacramental preparation, and more personal efforts for welcoming newcomers. Many estranged Catholics will be met in these ministries. It is important that we do them well—with inviting and inclusive attitudes and strategies.

I would also like to look at the Reconciling Community process critically. I have been a resource for many parishes around the country. I have written about it. And I have taught it at several graduate schools.

Some parishes that try to offer a weekly session for reconciliation experience a lot of coming and going—people who show up but don't return for some time. This is to be expected. This ministry has parallels with Alcoholics Anonymous, which also experiences a lot of coming and going based on the addict's motivation or the stage of healing and growth. I also believe that, as in AA, the quality of sponsoring can positively or negatively influence the regularity with which a returnee attends meetings.

Directly related to the "regularity" issue, or the quality of attendance, is the length of the process. I feel there is much to be learned from the revised Rite of Christian Initiation. In speaking of people seeking the sacraments of initiation, the revised text encourages parishes to be a constant posture of precatechumenate. In other words, instead of just running a program from fall to spring—a program to which the people must conform—the parish should be always welcoming people who come to the community. There ought to be ministers ready and trained to do ongoing inquiry, ready to help people whenever they come. Then, when these new people are ready, they can be merged into the larger catechumenal community on its journey toward Easter. The same can be said for reconciling those returning to the Church. In summary, the length of time for this process of reconciliation is truly a variable, dependent on unique circumstances and individuals.

This book is written to be pastoral in nature. So, I would like to add one more pastoral strategy that is working quite well. In the June 13, 1987, issue of *America*, there was an article entitled "Alienated Catholics Anonymous." The article described an approach used by Msgr. Thomas P. Cahalane. It is not the same approach as that of Father John Forliti, which I described briefly in chapter 7. It takes some of those insights, however, and gives them a Tucson, Arizona, and Irish spin. Cahalane offers a process of return at least twice a year, beginning on Christmas and on Easter. He feels that on these two days, we have a ready audience of inactive Catholics, some of whom may be ready to return to the Table of the Lord.

Cahalane always keeps focused on the participants' needs, questions, and hurts—on *their* agenda. There are some standard topics, however, that he considers basic.

1. Personal conversion
2. Reconciliation both in life and also through the sacramental celebration
3. Human sexuality and morality
4. The Eucharist and Catholic prayer and devotion
5. Marriage, divorce, and annulment
6. Ministry and service

Part of the process is the celebration of reconciliation and a special "teaching Mass" during which he explains the various elements of the renewed liturgy. The process lasts a maximum of six sessions. Cahalane uses a team approach, incorporating the personal witness of others who have recently completed the process.

Some who have completed the process speak briefly during Mass on Christmas and Easter. It is they who give the invitation to the process. There is a ritual of return during one of the Sunday Masses after the six sessions are completed. But only those who are comfortable with this public show of their reconciliation participate. A Prodigal Son and Daughter dinner celebrates the return of the inactive Catholics. Another key element is placing those who have returned in a ministry, a parish program, or some other form of active participation in the parish. Cahalane, and those commenting on this ministry, report great success with this approach.

What Msgr. Cahalane is doing is a kind of ongoing pre-catechumenate for those who have become estranged from the church family. Using the recent returnees to form the team for the next reconciling experience is also a form of ongoing conversion and reconciliation for them.

Recently, some of my students at Chicago's Loyola Institute for Pastoral Studies looked critically both at Cahalane's model and at my "Remember, Return, and Rebirth" process. The students felt that Cahalane's model is nonthreatening. It permits people to go on to other sessions after the six if they so desire. It is more congruent with people's internal calls and has a sense of immediacy which makes it attractive to busy people.

On the other hand, these students valued the process, companionship, storytelling, Scripture sharing, attentiveness to the liturgical year, and the Holy Thursday celebration reminiscent of the early Church that are all part of "Remember, Return, and Rebirth." The students' conclusion was that perhaps having two or three groups moving through a process of reconciliation during a year is a good idea. In such circumstances, no one need return until or unless he or she feels ready. People also should be able to have more than six sessions if they so desire. To illustrate that point, participants in Msgr. Cahalane's process are asking him to add more sessions. It is interesting to note that this request is coming from the people and not just from the staff.

In either case, Holy Thursday can be preserved as a day celebrating the return, the reconciliation of all who have returned to the Table of the Lord during the past year, and the reconciliation of any other parishioners who have chosen to participate as penitents during Lent.

One Illinois parish I have worked with is moving on to this hybrid model of the process. Another cluster of parishes which I serve as a consultant is implementing a year-long process. Still another suburban parish in the Chicago area is celebrating the reconciliation of all penitents at the Holy Week reconciliation service, but this parish reserves the "reverencing the Table" ritual for returning Catholics at the Holy Thursday liturgy.

I conclude with some of these models and adaptations to encourage you to be flexible and innovative in the way you use the ideas in this book for your own local circumstances.

There are two extremes to be avoided in the reconciliation process. On the one hand, be careful not to become too legalistic and elitist or too insistent on an unnecessarily long period of time for the process. This will turn off people who are genuinely excited about returning. On the other hand, be careful not to look for the quick fix that fails to effect real conversion and reconciliation in the hearts of those who wish to remember, return, and be reborn.

APPENDIX
Adapting the RCIA for the Reconciling Parish Process

As many parishes around the country have discovered, it is not necessary for you to completely reinvent the wheel to establish the reconciliation process. They are adapting some of the rituals of the RCIA for use in this process. Such adaptations are to be used only if they are judged to be pastorally wise or helpful. The regulations of copyright and fair use prevent me from providing you with complete adaptations of the prayers and rituals, but the process is simple enough. This appendix will give you the highlights of the portions of the RCIA that are applicable to the reconciling process. Then, you can read over the prayers and rituals that are recommended. Finally, you can alter the language of the prayers to change from the language of initiation to that of reconciliation.

For these guidelines, I am using the revised *Rite of Christian Initiation of Adults,* Study Edition, United States Catholic Conference, 1988. This revised rite calls for clear distinctions in public assemblies between the unbaptized, those baptized and seeking full communion with the Roman Catholic Church, the already baptized but uncatechized, and children of catechetical age.

Part II, section 4, of the Study Edition is entitled "Preparation of Uncatechized Adults for Confirmation and Eucharist." It offers new optional rites that also may be studied for the purposes of adaption for ministering in a reconciling community. Here are some of the parallels to the reconciliation rite:

1. What we call the Rite of Entrance is called the Rite of Welcoming the Candidates.

2. Parallel to our Ash Wednesday beginning of the Order of Penitents could be the Call to Ongoing Conversion and the Community's Act of Recognition.

3. A model for sending returnees or penitents to a general gathering with the bishop, or to meet with other people from neighboring parishes, can be found in the Rite of Sending the Candidates for Recognition by the Bishop.

4. A penitential rite is suggested for the baptized uncatechized for the second Sunday in Lent (or sometime during that week). This rite may be adapted and used instead of the scrutinies or exorcisms.

Here is an approach to doing the adaptations. First read the descriptions for each adaption given below. Then read through the prayers and rituals. Use a highlighting pen to mark those words and phrases that specifically relate to initiation. Substitute words and phrases more appropriate for reconciliation. For example, substitute the word *penitent* for *catechumen*. Phrases like "initiate them into your holiness" can become "restore them to your holiness." Many of the prayers demand little or no adaptation. Others will need more creative work on your part. Choose those prayers with which you or your ministers of sanctification are most comfortable.

Below are more specific guidelines for some of the elements in the RCIA which may be adapted for the reconciling process. Included are the minor exorcisms, the blessing of catechumens (penitents), the anointings, the scrutinies and exorcisms, the presentations, and the penitential rites. Please remember: The word *penitents* refers to the returnees (those returning to the Table of the Lord) as well as anyone else who has seriously engaged in the process of the Order of Penitents, which begins on Ash Wednesday.

MINOR EXORCISMS

The minor exorcisms are celebrated by a priest or a deacon, or by a worthy and suitable catechist delegated for this ministry. The celebrant extends his or her hands over the penitents, who bow or kneel. Then he or she says one or two of the prayers of exorcism (RCIA #93, A-K).

These exorcisms may take place anywhere the groups are meeting—church, hall, homes, or the like. They may be part of a Scripture service. They may be held at the beginning or end of a gathering for study. They may also be done privately. During the reconciling process, these exorcisms may be used more than once.

BLESSING OF PENITENTS

These blessings are found in RCIA #96, A-I. They are special signs of love and affection for the penitents given by the community. The blessings may be given by a priest, a deacon, or a catechist. The celebrant extends his or her hands toward the penitents and offers one or two of the blessing prayers. After the prayers, the penitents come to the celebrant. The celebrant then lays hands on each penitent. The penitents may then leave. Again, the pastoral question of whether penitents (including returnees) should be dismissed after the Liturgy of the Word is a hot debate around the country.

The blessings are usually given at the end of the Liturgy of the Word. They may also be given at the end of a gathering for instruction. If there are special needs, the blessings may be given privately to individual penitents. There is no special time during the stages of the process for these blessings. They can be used any time for the spiritual good of the penitents.

ANOINTINGS

If it seems desirable to strengthen the penitents with an anointing, the first anointing of catechumens may be adapted for this purpose. (See RCIA #98-#103.) The anointing can be given by a priest, a deacon, a catechist, or a delegated minister. It is best celebrated after the homily in the Liturgy of the Word. The anointing can be given to all the penitents. For special reasons, it may also be given privately to individual penitents. The anointing should be an encouragement to the penitents to continue on the journey of reconciliation.

SCRUTINIES AND EXORCISMS

The scrutinies have a spiritual purpose. They are intended to purify the penitents' minds and hearts, to strengthen them against temptation, to purify their intentions, and to make firm their decision. These rituals are meant to help the penitents stay closely united with Christ and make progress in their efforts to love God.

The rite of exorcism is celebrated by a priest or a deacon. In this rite, the Church teaches people about the mystery of Christ who frees them from sin. The exorcisms are not to be treated superstitiously. But by these special prayers, people are helped to be freed from the effects of sin and from the influences of evil. They are strengthened in their spiritual journey and are made open to the gifts of the Spirit.

Scrutinies take place at the Mass on the third, fourth, and fifth Sundays of Lent. The readings and chants from series A are used. If, for pastoral reasons, these scrutinies cannot be celebrated on the proper Sundays, other Lenten Sundays or even weekdays may be chosen. The reading for the first scrutiny is always that of the Samaritan woman; the second, of the man born blind; and the third, of Lazarus being raised from the dead.

Below is a thumbnail guide to the scrutinies. Be sure that there is no confusion between penitents and catechumens in the celebration of the scrutinies. There is a dramatic difference in status among the unbaptized being received into the Church, regular members of the Church on a path of public penance, and once-alienated members in the process of return.

1. **First Scrutiny.** See RCIA #150–#156. Substitute the word *penitent* for the word *elect*. Use option A for the intercessions for the elect. Be careful of the introductory prayer. You may want to provide a simple and extemporaneous introduction to the intercessions. Also use option A for the exorcism; it is the easiest to adapt. In the summary prayer, use the language of return to the Father and faith. Do not dismiss the penitents at this time. Go on to the general intercessions, one of which mentions the returnees.

2. **Second Scrutiny.** See RCIA #164–#170. The introduction to the intercessions is quite simple to adapt. Option A for the

intercessions can be used with almost no changes. Use form B for the exorcism. But go back to form A for the summary prayer. Do not dismiss the penitents. Go to the general intercessions, but include at least one petition that specifically mentions the penitents, including returnees.

3. Third Scrutiny. See RCIA #171–#176. In the opening prayer, pray that the "grace of reconciliation conform them to Christ. ..." Use option B for the intercessions, but skip the fourth and fifth intercessions. Use option A for the exorcism, but be a bit careful of the summary prayer. Again, include the penitents in the general intercessions.

PRESENTATIONS

The presentations of the Profession of Faith, or Creed (RCIA #157–#163), and of the Lord's Prayer (#178–#184) are usually celebrated after the scrutinies during the third and fifth weeks of Lent. However, they may be celebrated before the usual Lenten setting because they may be of more benefit during the time of faith formation. Moreover, Lent is short and already has a great deal of activity crammed into it. The presentations should be celebrated when the penitents seem ready for them. With the formation of the penitents completed or well under way, the Church restores to them two important markers: a summary of our faith (the Creed) and Jesus' model prayer (the Lord's Prayer).

The reconciling community can decide a good time and place for these presentations. It is customary in some parishes to actually present an attractive printed copy of the Creed and the Lord's Prayer. However, I have found that saying or praying the Creed and the Lord's Prayer line by line, with the catechumens (in the RCIA) or the penitents (in this process) facing the faith community and repeating each line, is a more powerful handing on of these two articulations of faith.

The following hints may help you adapt the presentations to the reconciliation process.

1. The Creed. See RCIA #157–#163. For the second reading the passage from 1 Corinthians (shorter version) is better for this purpose. For the Gospel, choose the reading from John. As you introduce the presentation (#160), go into some detail about renewing the penitents, including returnees, in this statement of faith. Use the Nicene Creed. You should compose your own prayer over the penitents (#161).

2. The Lord's Prayer.   See RCIA #178–#184. Choose the reading from Romans. The presentation of the Lord's Prayer *is* the Gospel reading, but it would be good to elaborate on the introduction (#181) in order to put it in the context of the reconciliation process. The Prayer over the Elect (#182) does not fit the reconciliation process at all. It would be best to compose a prayer especially for this purpose. Follow the form of the prayer given in the rite.

PENITENTIAL RITES

There are some who feel that adapting the scrutinies and exorcisms for returnees is not as effective as adapting the penitential rite of the Second Sunday of Lent, found in #464–#472 of the revised rite. The revised rite also speaks of the liturgical distribution of Bibles and crosses, both of which may help in the journey back to the Table. Some of the language of the revised rite, like "the call to conversion," is more appropriate language than speaking of a rite of election, when the returnees enter the Order of Penitents at the beginning of Lent.

INDEX

Adult religious education, 38–42
African model, for studying Scripture, 71
Alienated Catholics, categories of, 6–10
  adolescents, 6–7
  children, 6
  racial-ethnic dropouts, 7–8
  uninvolved active members, 8–9
  young adults, 7
Alienated Catholics Anonymous, 69–70
"Alienated Catholics Anonymous," 108
Alienated Protestants, 12
Alienation, reasons for, 4–6
Andragogy, 38
Annulment, 24–25
Anointing of the Sick, 95
Anointings, 57, 113
Ash Wednesday, 53–55
Australia, the Church in, 2–3

Baptism, 15, 62–63, 94
Bates, Marilyn, 46
Becker, Ernest, 100
Bellah, Robert, 13
Blackoll, John, 26

Bloom, Allan, 46, 83
Boff, Leonardo, 13

Cahalane, Thomas P., 108–9
Castelli, James, 7, 9
Catechesis, for returning members, 67–73
  participants' experiences, 68–70
  praying and studying Scriptures, 70–72
Catechumenate, 6
Catholicism, American, 11–12
Catholics. *See also* Alienated Catholics
  Asian, 8
  divorced, 24–25
  first church, 1
  Hispanic, 7–8
  returning, 26, 40–42, 67–73
  second church, 1–2
  third church, 2, 4
Chicago, archdiocese of, 4
Church, one, holy, catholic, apostolic, reflection on, 90–91
Community, Christian, 12–14
Confirmation, 64–65, 94
Creed, 42, 58, 72–73, 115–16
  sessions for studying, 75–105

Discernment, 50
Dismissals, 58–59
Divorce, 24–25
Dominian, Jack, 1
Dulles, Avery, 41–42, 90
Durkin, Mary Greeley, 13

Eucharist, 94–95
Evangelization
　cycle of, 27–29
　period of, 48
Evangelizing Parish, The, 4
Exorcisms, 58, 114
　minor, 112–13

First Eucharist, 63
First Reconciliation, 64
Fitzpatrick, James M., 2–3
Flores, Patrick, 26
Forliti, John, 69–70
Fowler, James, 46
Full Gospel Central Church, Seoul, Korea, 14

Gallup, George, 7, 9
German Catechetical Association, 70
Gestalt therapy, 68
Greeley, Andrew, 13
Groome, Thomas, 39–40

Herzog, Frederick, 12, 14
Hoge, Dean, 26
Holy Orders, 95
Holy Spirit, reflection on, 84–85
Holy Thursday, 20, 49, 50, 55–57
Hornsby-Smith, Michael, 1
Hurston, John and Karen, 14

Internal forum, 24–25

James, William, 6
Jehovah's Witnesses, 26
Jesus, God's Son, our Lord, reflection on, 81–82

Keirsey, David, 46
Kemp, Ray, 72
Kushner, Harold, 76

Lectionary, 42, 71
Legalism, 32
Lobinger, Fritz, 40
Loder, James, 34
Lopresti, James J., 20, 37
Lord's Prayer, 58, 115, 116
Lumko Institute, 40, 72

McBrien, Richard, 70
McCready, William, 11
Manipulation, 32
Marriage, 65, 95
Marthaler, Bernard, 70
Marty, Martin, 9, 13
Mary, mother of Jesus, reflection on, 87–88
Mass, attendance at, 11
Michael, Chester P., 46
Ministers
　of accompaniment, 42–44
　of sanctification, prayer, and liturgy, 45–46
　of the Word, 37–42
Mormon Church, 26
Mystagogical gathering, 50
Mystery, reflection on, 75–76

Newcomers, process for welcoming, 47, 59–61
Norrisey, Marie C., 46

Order of Penitents, vii–viii, 16, 53–55
Ostling, Richard N., 7–8

Parks, Sharon, 34, 46
Pedagogy, 38
Penitential rites, 116
Penitents
　blessing of, 113
　title and identity of, 23–24, 53
Perls, Fritz, 68
Personal relationships, 26–27
Prayer, 45–46
Preevangelization, 19, 43, 50
Presbyterian Church, 27
Presentations
　the Creed, 58, 115–16
　the Lord's Prayer, 58, 115, 116
　the Scriptures, 58

Proselytizing, 26–27
Protestant churches, mainline, 12, 26
Provost, James, 25

Quindlen, Donna, 4

Ramirez, Ricardo, 26
Reconciliation
  existential, 17
  experiencing, 17
  process view of, 15–16
  sacrament of, 15, 95
Reconciling community process,
    18–21, 27–29, 47–50
  commitment, 19–20
  critique of, 107–10
  Easter celebration, 21
  evangelization period, 48
  follow-up, 49
  formation period, 48
  Holy Thursday celebration, 49
  Lenten penitential season, 49
  national meeting on, 43
  ongoing evangelization, 21
  outreach and preevangelization,
    19
  purification, 20–21
  RCIA adapted for, 111–16
  sample services, 50–59
  sharing of stories, 19
Reconversion, process of, 15
Resurrection, reflection on, 100–102
Revivals, 27
Rite of Christian Initiation of Adults
    (RCIA), vii–viii, 16
RCIA process
  adapting, 111–16
  principles underlying, 32–34
  separate but parallel, 31–32
  tools in, 34–35
Rite of Entrance, 50–53
Rituals, 34

Sacramental preparation, 47, 61–65
Sacraments, reflection on, 93–96
Saint Augustine Church,
    Washington, D.C., 72
Saint John the Evangelist Parish,
    Chicago suburb, 19
Savage, John, 4–5, 68–69
Scriptures
  praying and studying, 70–72
  presentation of, 58
Scrutinies, 58, 114–15
Second Coming, reflection on, 103–4
Sheehy, Gail, 101
Sin, reflection on, 97–98
Solidarity, 14–15
Southern Baptist Convention, 26
Sponsors, 42–45
Stewardship, 11
Storytelling, 34–35, 69
Sweetser, Thomas, 4
Symbols, 34, 35

Teilhard de Chardin, Pierre, 103
Trinity, reflection on, 78–79

United Methodist Church, 27

van Kaam, Adrian, 46

Warren, Michael, 7, 43–44, 67
Whitehead, James and Evelyn, 39, 40